MIND YOUR LOGIC

**Second Edition
Revised Printing**

Donald R. Gregory

Northern Virginia Community College – Annandale

Kendall Hunt
publishing company

Back cover photo courtesy of Mary Gregory

Kendall Hunt
publishing company

www.kendallhunt.com
Send all inquiries to:
4050 Westmark Drive
Dubuque, IA 52004-1840

ISBN 978-1-4652-1283-2

Printed in the United States of America
10 9 8 7

To my wife Mary
and my family:
Chris, Mary Katherine, Katie, Henry and Sam
Geoff and Jesse
Frank and Anna

*For showing me in countless ways
That there's more to life than logic*

Contents

Preface

Sometimes it is helpful to reflect upon how we do the things we do. Reasoning logically is one of the things we do, and in this book we will reflect upon how we do it. How is it that some of the reasoning humans engage in is successful and some is not?

What makes a piece of reasoning logically successful? What are the criteria by which we judge this success?

Mind Your Logic is intended to answer these and similar questions. Designed for the introductory logic student, it is essentially the course I have taught to several thousand students at George Mason University, at Northern Virginia Community College, and in a distance education format online and by cable television at other colleges. It contains a treatment of the essential ingredients of an introductory course: the nature, strengths, and limitations of logic; induction vs. deduction; the relation between language and logic; informal fallacies; the classical logic of the categorical proposition and categorical syllogism; symbolic or truth-functional logic including the truth-table method of testing arguments, formal proof of validity, and a brief introduction to quantification. Exercises are provided for each major point covered, and in addition to traditional "problem-solving" exercises, there are many invitations to the student to explain in a brief paragraph the concept just discussed. This latter sort of exercise is designed to provide a "reality check" to be sure the student is not simply memorizing formulas and definitions. Working through the exercises serves the dual purpose of providing practice in careful writing and learning key logical concepts in other than a rote manner. Answers to all the exercises in the text, in addition to some extra exercises for pratice, will be found at the end of the book.

Some distinctive features of the book include the following:

1. Emphasis is given to the role logic plays in our lives with regard to both its strengths and limitations. Students often enter a logic course with unrealistic expectations. They want to learn whether it is *logical* to believe or disbelieve in God, whether abortion is or is not a *logical* moral choice, etc. Considerable attention is given to divesting them of the opinion that logic alone can decide these weighty matters for them. At the

same time, the absolutely essential role which logic must play in any rational attempt to deal with these and similar questions is stressed. The book begins and ends with discussions of the nature and place of logic.

2. Analogies are frequently employed to make difficult concepts easier to understand. To cite one example, the key role of the middle term in a categorical syllogism is illustrated by considering two strangers who have a common friend. Any relationship between the two strangers is, at least initially, mediated or facilitated by the common friend. Similarly, any conclusion of a categorical syllogism which shows a relationship between the minor and major terms will be mediated by the middle term. These and similar analogies have been honed over years of classroom teaching and, while not perfect, can be certified as effective in making the point.

3. Philosophical controversies in logic, while not ignored, are mentioned only briefly for what they are, namely issues which primarily concern professionals and advanced students in the field. Examples of such controversies include: how best to translate singular propositions (e.g. "Socrates is a man") into categorical propositions, how the problem of existential import affects the drawing of Venn Diagrams and the interpretation of the rules of syllogistic inference, the precise distinction between statements and propositions, etc. The strategy in this book is simple and straightforward. Where philosophical issues lurk just beneath the surface of a given point or concept, the student is so advised in a brief comment or two. Care is taken, however, not to interrupt the point or concept under consideration.

My wife and colleague, Mary S. Gregory, has read the entire manuscript and has greatly clarified its organization and content both in my mind and on the printed page. She also solved, in approximately five minutes, the question of a title for the book, something I had pondered for three years. My friend and colleague Dan Rothbart has read and offered helpful suggestions on portions of the book. In addition, several thousand students over the years have patiently heard, questioned, and thus helped me refine, many of the presentations of topics and issues. My son Geoff Gregory became the first student to use the book; his suggestions have mercifully eased the burden on his successors. Despite all this help, inadequacies remain, and these must be attributed to the author.

Chantilly, Virginia
January, 2013

CHAPTER ONE

What Logic Is and Is Not

1.1 What Logic Can and Cannot Do

Logic is an area of study which is often misunderstood. It is typical, in an introductory logic class, for first-day questions to include something like the following:

1. Will I learn how to think logically?
2. Will I find out, once and for all, whether God exists?
3. Will I discover whether abortion is moral?

Such questions illustrate the need for studying logic primarily because they show that it is not clear to most people what logic is, what it can and cannot do. Let's examine the questions in turn:

1. Hopefully anyone who completes a logic course will be better at reasoning logically than he or she was previously. This is not, however, because the course has somehow imparted an ability which previously was not there—the ability "to think logically." Any adult who makes it as far as taking a college course, or selecting and reading a book, or for that matter living through a single day in a busy life, is already capable of thinking logically. Not that we all think logically all of the time, but by and large those of us who live ordinary human lives must of necessity think logically a good deal of the time. The goal in studying logic is not so much to learn how to think logically, as to learn what it is that makes the logical thinking we already do work successfully. Our job, in other words, is more like that of the centipede which, when asked how it could walk with its hundred legs, became so confused that it could no longer walk. Fortunately for us, we are endowed with enough mental capacity that the prospects for examining how we do what we do are somewhat brighter.

2. Many people are convinced that great issues such as whether God exists can be resolved if only we could be logical. It is very typical, for example, for someone to think that the alternative he or she prefers is the "logical" one and that everyone who disagrees is "illogical." Thus, to many atheists, those who believe in God are not logical, and to many theists (believers in God), it is their opponents who are illogical. The problem with this way of looking at such issues is, of course, that historically there are great thinkers who have expended much energy defending both sides of the issue. If a certain position really were illogical, one would be hard-put to find serious thinkers who defended it. The fact is that logical arguments can be given for the existence of God, but logical arguments can also be given for the non-existence of God. Logic does not reveal to us a realm of truth, though logic is certainly essential for the success of any attempt to discover the truth.

3. Similarly when it comes to moral issues, to "oughts" as philosophers like to call them, many would say that logic can be used to show that a given action such as abortion is never moral, or sometimes moral, or always moral. Here things are a bit more tricky, because it is not clear that any moral injunction (e.g. "You ought to do so-and-so") ever follows logically from purely factual statements (e.g. "Such-and-such is the case"). Philosophers call this the "is-ought" problem. Assuming without further discussion that moral injunctions can follow from purely factual statements, then one can show that all of the alternatives above are "logical." Many people think that their moral view is the "logical" one while the other side is "illogical." But once again, the more serious thinkers on all sides of such moral issues as abortion are certainly capable of logical thinking. Thus, depending upon whom we talk to, abortion can be shown logically to have any status from morally praiseworthy to morally reprehensible.

The above raises the obvious questions of the nature and value of logic. In a sense all of this book will attempt to answer these questions, but it is high time we begin with at least a provisional answer. **Logic can be defined as the study of the techniques we use to distinguish good from bad reasoning.** Virtually everyone is capable of good reasoning, and most of us do reason well a good deal of the time. But we are also capable of bad reasoning, we sometimes engage in it, and if nothing else we are frequently subjected to it. So it is important to be able to tell whether a piece of reasoning is any good or not. In studying logic, we are studying the techniques that can be used to assess a piece of reasoning. We are not concerned with why some people reason better than others, nor with what happens either psychologically or physiologically when we reason. Logic is not, in other words, concerned with psychology, or sociology, or neurophysiology.

1.2 Arguments

Logic deals with the form of reasoning, not the content. To illustrate what this means, consider the following classical argument, found in nearly every book ever written on logic:

> All humans are mortal.
> Socrates is human.
> Therefore, Socrates is mortal.

One does not need to take a logic course to see, more or less intuitively, that this is a good piece of reasoning. We will see, eventually, precisely why this is so, but we can note for the present that the logical success of this reasoning does not depend upon, for example, whether all humans really are mortal or not, or whether Socrates really is human, or for that matter, whether Socrates really is mortal. If it should be discovered that there never was a Socrates, the logical success of this reasoning would be unaffected. This is what it means to say that the content of the reasoning—what it talks about, and whether what it talks about is true—does not affect its logical success. Rather, the form or structure or pattern of the reasoning is what makes it logically successful. To see very roughly what the form is, remove the content-words "humans," "mortal," and "Socrates," and replace them with letters H, M, and S. Then we have:

> All H are M.
> S is H.
> Therefore, S is M.

This is the form of the piece of reasoning we are considering, and what makes this reasoning successful is the way the terms (H, M, and S) work together. They work in a hypothetical or an "if-then" way: Whatever H, M, and S might stand for, if all H are M, and S is an H, then S would have to be M. This is what we will soon be able to call a valid deductive argument, one typical kind of "good" reasoning. But before we can fully appreciate what this means, we need to define some terms.

What we have described above as a "piece of reasoning" is really called an "argument." Logic takes many ordinary words such as "argument," "valid," "true," etc. and uses them in a very precise way. When logicians talk about arguments they do not mean anything unpleasant such as shouting or fisticuffs or calling the police. **An argument, as logicians define the term, is simply a series of statements such that one of them (the conclusion) is said to follow from the others (the premisses).** Thus the argument above has two premisses ("All H are M" and "S is

H") and a conclusion ("S is M"). "S is M" is said to follow from the premisses (this is why the word "therefore" is used), and the premisses, in turn, are said to provide evidence, or reasons, for accepting the conclusion. By definition, any single argument contains only one conclusion, though it is entirely possible for a single paragraph of writing to contain numerous arguments. The conclusion of a given argument can, for example, become a premiss in a brand new argument. "Socrates is mortal," the conclusion of our original argument above, could be combined with another statement such as "All mortals will die," to produce a new conclusion, "Socrates will die." In this new argument, "Socrates is mortal" is a premiss, whereas it was previously a conclusion. The terms "premiss" and "conclusion," then, are relative to the argument in which the statements appear. A statement all by itself is simply a statement, but in a given argument that statement might give evidence for some other statement and thus be a premiss. Or it might be said to follow from one or more other statements and thus be a conclusion. There is nothing unusual about this: consider other similar terms such as "student" and "teacher." In certain situations I am a teacher, but in others I might be a student. Outside the teaching/learning setting, I am just me. The same goes for terms such as father/son, mother/daughter, employer/employee, etc.

Though arguments by definition have only one conclusion each, the number of premisses has no upper limit. As a minimum there must, of course, be one premiss. (A conclusion cannot be said "to follow" from nothing.) The argument above has two premisses, as will the majority of the arguments we will be considering. Sometimes, however, an argument can have many more premisses, and occasionally the number of premisses is actually open-ended. Consider the conclusion, "It always rains the day after I wash my car." The premisses are countless, encompassing past, present and (at least by implication) future.

There are big differences in the way arguments are stated. When a logician is preparing to analyze the logic of an argument, he or she always states the argument in a formal, structured way. Normally, the premisses are stated first and in a certain order, followed by the conclusion. Often the symbol ∴ is used to indicate the conclusion; the rough translation of this symbol is "therefore." Much of what we will do in this book involves formally stating and analyzing arguments to see whether their conclusions follow from their premisses. Most of the time, however, we encounter arguments in contexts other than the formal study of logic. In ordinary language, there are a variety of ways in which arguments may be stated. Let us take the argument above to illustrate these ways:

1. Sometimes we state the conclusion first, followed by the premisses, e.g.: "Socrates is mortal, because all humans are mortal and Socrates is human." Here we use a word like "because" to show that we are about to give reasons or evidence for the conclusion. Other words and expres-

sions which indicate that the premisses are about to be given include "since," "as," "for," "for the reason(s) that," "is shown by," etc.

2. Sometimes we "sandwich" the conclusion in the middle of an argument, e.g.: "All humans are mortal, so Socrates is mortal, since he's human." Note the word "so" which indicates that the words to follow are the conclusion. Other words and expressions which indicate that a conclusion is coming include "therefore," "thus," "hence," "accordingly," "for these reasons," "it follows that," etc. Note also that it would be rather awkward in a short argument like the above to repeat the name of Socrates twice; the pronoun "he" is used the second time Socrates is mentioned.

3. Sometimes we do indeed state the premisses followed by the conclusion, just as we must do in a formal logical statement of an argument. It is not unusual to hear the above argument stated conversationally as follows: "All humans are mortal, and Socrates is human, so he's mortal." Again the word "so" is used to indicate the conclusion.

4. Sometimes one of the premisses, or even the conclusion, is so obvious that it is not even stated. Imagine a discussion on ancient culture in which someone asks whether Socrates was one of the immortal gods of Greek mythology. Another person might reply, "Oh, no, Socrates was human, so he was mortal." In this context it is obvious to everyone that all humans are mortal. We give the Greek name **enthymeme** to an argument which has an unstated premiss or conclusion.

In ordinary language, we often do not use indicators because the premisses and the conclusion are clear without them. Other times it is not so clear; ordinary language is notorious for its vagueness at times. The general question the logician must ask is, "Is it clear what this speaker or writer wants me to believe?" If so, this is the conclusion; the premisses are the reasons he or she gives to try to convince me that the conclusion is true. What if, after reasonable consideration, we cannot figure out what the point of this particular piece of speaking or writing is? That is, we cannot decide what is the conclusion, what are the premisses, or perhaps whether there is an argument here at all. (Much speaking and writing does not contain arguments.) In this case our job as logician cannot be done; we cannot analyze the logical correctness of an argument when we cannot tell what the argument is. This is not our problem, assuming again that we have made an effort; it is the problem of the speaker or writer of the passage in question.

Imagine that you are the computer operator for a small business. Your job is to take the requests of the various offices in the business and process them using the company computer. Different offices give you their requests in different formats; sometimes neatly filled-out forms, sometimes scribbled notes, sometimes forms with scribbled notes, etc. You are pretty good at figuring out these requests, and can normally put the needed information into the formal language of the computer. Sometimes, though, it is just not clear to you what is being asked. Your job, at this point, is not to try to read the minds of those who gave you the request; your job is to run the computer. You will therefore send back the occasional vague request with a note asking for clarification or more information.

What logic does is similar in many ways to what a computer does, including the fact that both have a formal language (or rather, several formal languages) which they use, and without which they cannot function. We will shortly be exploring other similarities.

1.3 Statements and Sentences

In the discussion of arguments so far we have used the term "statement" as though it were perfectly obvious what a statement is. In fact, a good deal of work has been done by philosophers, linguists, and logicians, especially in the twentieth century, on the very question of defining the term "statement."[1] While the subtleties of this discussion are beyond the scope of this book, what follows is a brief summary of what comes as close to being a consensus as philosophers tend to come on these issues.

A statement is a claim or assertion that something is or is not so. If I say "The book is on the table" I have made a statement because I have claimed that the book is on the table. All statements are either true or false, true if what they say is so really is so, false otherwise. So if there really is a book on the table, then my statement is true; otherwise it is false.

It is not always possible, of course, to determine right here and now whether a statement really is true or false. A statement about the future, for example, must wait to be checked. A statement about a book on a table in some other room, or in some other part of the world, is similarly impossible to confirm right here and now. What is important, though, is that we can agree on what it would take to show whether these statements are true or false. There is what some philosophers have called a "verification procedure": an agreement about what sort of observation would count as evidence for or against the truth of the statement. The fact that we cannot make the observation right now does not mean that we cannot agree on what observation would be relevant if we could make it. Take the statement, "The population of Mon-

---

[1] Throughout this book, the terms "statement" and "proposition" will be used synonymously. There are differences which become important at the more advanced levels of logic, but these will not concern us here. The term "statement" will be used in this introductory chapter, while "proposition" will be used primarily in reference to Aristotelian logic in Chapter Three.

tana will be 1,200,000 in the year 2020." This is either true or false, but we will not know until 2020 which it is. We can agree right now, however, on a verification procedure for this statement: a census of Montana in the year 2020.

Many philosophers claim that any utterance, piece of writing, or other purported statement which has no verification procedure is not a statement at all. A.J. Ayer, one of the pioneers in the philosophical analysis of logic, called such utterances "literal nonsense." In *Language, Truth, and Logic* (1936), Ayer attacks ethical, religious, and metaphysical utterances, among others, as not being genuine statements.[2] His work here played a pivotal role in what was one of the great philosophical debates of the twentieth century. What is important for our purposes now, however, is to distinguish statements from the sentences used to express or assert them.

All the statements we have used in our examples so far have been expressed in written sentences. "The book is on the table," for example, is a written sentence which expresses a statement. A moment's thought will show, however, that the sentence is not the same thing as the statement. The identical statement could be made with the sentence, "On the table there is a book." This is clearly a different sentence from the first one, yet just as clearly the statement made is the same. One can think of the sentence as the means whereby the statement gets expressed or made, rather in the way a car is the vehicle that carries you from place to place. Let's say your good friend Joe always drives a brown Chevy. When you see the brown Chevy coming you might well say, "Here comes Joe." All you see is the car, but you so identify the car with Joe that it is natural to say, "Here comes Joe." Of course, someone else could very well be driving Joe's car today, and it is just as possible that Joe could arrive in a different car, or on a bus, or whatever. You don't seriously think that Joe and the car are the same thing. Similarly, sentences and statements are different in several ways:

1. As noted above, sometimes two or more sentences can express the same statement. "There is a book on the table" and "On the table there is a book" are two sentences asserting a single statement. In addition to having a different word order, sentences in different languages also serve as an example; so do sentences using synonyms, e.g.: "Jane is a lawyer" and "Jane is an attorney."

2. Sometimes two or more statements can be expressed by the same sentence. As an example, consider a sentence such as "There is a book

---

[2] Actually, Ayer says that there are two kinds of meaningful statements. In addition to those that are verifiable, there are what he calls "analytic" statements. These are either true or false due to the meaning of their terms. "All bachelors are unmarried" is analytically true and "No bachelors are unmarried" is analytically false. For Ayer, then, utterances which look like statements but are **neither verifiable nor analytic** are "literal nonsense."

here." I might utter that sentence while pointing to a bookshelf, or to a table, or to a desk, or whatever. The context would determine what place is referred to by the word "here." And depending upon what the place is, this single sentence might make any number of different statements, e.g., "There is a book on the bookshelf," "There is a book on the table," "There is a book on the desk," etc. Just as sentences containing words designating places (e.g. "here" and "there") can make different statements, so can sentences designating times. Consider the sentence, "It is early in the morning now." When that sentence is uttered at 6:00AM, it makes a very different statement than when it is uttered at 6:00PM. The word "now" refers to the present time, and since 6:00AM and 6:00PM are two very different times of day, the statements made are very different. They are so different, in fact, that when one of them is true the other is false.

3. Sometimes statements are made without the use of sentences at all. We have all observed certain looks that make strong statements! Gestures, nods, even silence, can all be used to make statements. A teacher might get a non-talkative class to begin discussing issues by saying something like, "I assume that your silence means this is all perfectly clear." An audience at a concert might make a strong statement by refusing to applaud—or by booing. Certainly feelings are being expressed in such cases, but statements are also being made (e.g., "This is a bad band").

4. Sometimes sentences do other things than make statements. We have all studied the four traditional kinds of sentences: declarative, imperative, interrogative, and exclamatory. Of these, only declarative sentences make statements, such as (again) "The book is on the table." Consider the others in turn:

>   Imperative sentences are commands such as "Stand up," "Forward march," or "Please close the window." They do not make statements because, first, they do not claim that anything is or is not so, and second, they are neither true nor false. Consider how odd it would be to comment, "Yes, that's true" after the sergeant calls, "Forward march." Commands are, of course, requests for action. "Forward march" requests that the troops march, and of course an observer might well make statements such as "They marched when asked to do so," "They are slow," "Their rows are crooked," or whatever. But "Forward march" itself is not a statement; it is a request for action.

Interrogative sentences, commonly called questions, are requests for information. "What is the name of this city?" "What time is it?" "Who is the person in charge of this department?" are all questions. Questions are not statements and thus do not make claims and are neither true nor false. When we answer a question, of course, we normally make a statement, e.g. "This is New York," "It's 9:00," "Mrs. Smith is the head of this department," etc.

One of the best ways to think of the difference between questions and statements is to consider how ridiculous it can be **not** to see the difference. The classic Abbott and Costello comedy routine, "Who's On First," is a wonderfully entertaining example of such confusion. Abbott is the manager of a baseball team on which the players have most unusual names. "Who" is the first baseman, "What" plays second base, and "I Don't Know" plays third. The other positions also have players with names similarly designed to confuse. Costello asks Abbott the question, "Who's on first?" Abbott takes this normally straightforward question as a statement, since he knows that "Who" is the name of the first basemen. Thus he says to Costello, "That's right." As a statement, "Who's on first" is right because "Who" is on first. But Costello, not knowing this, is completely befuddled (something not at all difficult for Costello) since he had asked a question. "That's right" is not an appropriate answer to a question, so he assumes that Abbott misunderstood and rephrases the question, "I mean what is the name of the player at first base?" Abbott, again taking his friend's question as a statement, this time says, "No, What is the name of the player at second base." As a statement, of course, that is correct. Costello, now completely frustrated, finally does make a statement: "I'm not asking you who's on second." With an air of impatience, Abbott responds, "Who's on first." Any reader who has not read or heard the entire routine should do so—it is one of the great pieces of radio and television comedy, and we can now begin to see why this is so.

The last of the four "traditional" kinds of sentence is the exclamatory. "Hooray!" "Boo!" "Right on!" and the like are exclamations, and sentences containing them are exclamatory sentences. The exclamations themselves do not make statements—"Hooray" is after all neither true nor false, nor does it assert or claim anything to be the case—but typically sentences containing such terms do go on to make statements. An example would be: "Hooray, our team won!" "Our team won" is either true or false regardless of whether it is preceded by "Hooray." "Hooray" serves to express the positive feelings and excitement of the speaker.

There is another kind of sentence which does not make a statement and which, nevertheless, is very similar to both statements and commands. This is the performative utterance. Recall that imperative sentences are commands which request that action take place. After the imperative sentence is uttered, the action takes place. The sergeant certainly expects the troops to march after he says, "Forward march." The sergeant's words themselves do not do the marching; they are the cause of the soldiers marching. In a performative utterance the words themselves perform the action. Consider "I promise to meet you tomorrow." To say this in the appropriate context is to promise to meet you tomorrow. The sentence performs the action of making a promise. Nothing further needs to happen to insure that a promise has been made. Of course, I may make a promise without intending to keep it, or I may sincerely make a promise but later find that I cannot keep it, but in both of these cases a promise has still been made. Ritual and parliamentary actions frequently contain performative utterances, e.g.: "The meeting is hereby adjourned," "I take this man/woman to be my husband/wife," "I do," "I move that we form a committee," "I second the motion," "I apologize," etc.

Just as we can get a clear look at the difference between statements and questions by examining a case where the two are ridiculously confused ("Who's on First"), so we can examine a similar case to see what a performative utterance is and is not. Put briefly, the context has to be clear; all parties have to understand that a performative utterance is being made. If a non-English-speaker is taught to utter, "I promise to pay you a million dollars," but has no idea what the words mean, one can hardly equate uttering the words with making a real promise. In the Jim Henson movie, *The Muppets Take Manhattan,* the closing scene shows the importance of a shared understanding of the context. Miss Piggy and Kermit the Frog are appearing in a Broadway production which culminates in their wedding. Both understand that this is only a play, but Miss Piggy, who has long wanted to marry Kermit for real, concocts a plot. At the point in the play where the wedding scene is to take place, Miss Piggy arranges for a real clergyman to appear. This is supposed to have the effect of making the ceremony real. When the real minister says to Kermit, "Do you, Froggie, take this Piggy . . . ?" Kermit realizes if he says, "I do," he will be making a performative utterance, not just giving his line in the play. He pauses for what seems forever, gulps, and then—knowing what his words are doing—says, "I do." This humorous example is echoed in the very common case of a wedding rehearsal, where all parties understand that the words are not "for real." When the same words are spoken at the wedding itself, such expressions as "I do," "I thee wed," "I pronounce you husband and wife," etc., are clearly performative utterances.

So statements and sentences are quite different things. The statement, again, is what is claimed or asserted in the sentence.

————————————— —————————————

Exercise: *Test your understanding of the above discussion by trying the following.*

I.   State in a paragraph or two some of the strengths and limitations of logic. Is logic of any value, despite its limitations? Share your answer with a fellow student or your instructor and discuss.

II.   Tell whether each of the following sentences is a: (a) statement; (b) question; (c) command; (d) performative utterance.

  1.   There is a book on the table.   *a*

  2.   Is there a book on the table?   *b*

  3.   Put a book on the table.   *c*

  4.   Why is there a book on the table?   *b*

  5.   I apologize for there being a book on the table.   *d* *?*

  6.   The sergeant said, "Forward march."   *c*

  7.   I promise to march when you say "Forward march."   *d*

  8.   Forward march.   *c*

  9.   Did the soldiers march?   *b*

  10. The soldiers did march.   *a*

1.4 Inductive and Deductive Arguments

Recall now that the above discussion concerning statements was an outgrowth of our definition of an argument as a series of statements such that one is said to follow from the others. There are two quite different kinds of arguments, and while they are well-known and frequently discussed, the precise difference between them is often misunderstood. The two kinds of arguments are deductive and inductive, and there is a "standard" definition of the difference between the two which runs like this: Deductive arguments move from very general or "universal" premises such as "All humans are mortal" to very specific or "particular" conclusions such as "Socrates is mortal." Inductive arguments do the opposite, moving from specific premises or "examples" of something (e.g. a list of humans each of whom is mortal) to a general conclusion such as "All humans are mortal." More often than not—and almost always in contexts outside of logic courses—one sees the difference between the two kinds of arguments defined in this way. Unfortunately, there are two very serious problems with this way of distinguishing the deductive and inductive arguments. First, this distinction simply doesn't apply to all the cases. There are many deductive arguments which do indeed move from general to specific as discussed, but there are many others which remain on the level of the general, e.g.:

> All humans are mortal.
> All mortals will die.
> Therefore, all humans will die.

Further, there are many deductive arguments which remain entirely on the level of the specific, e.g.:

> If Socrates is mortal, then Socrates will die.
> Socrates is mortal.
> Therefore, Socrates will die.

When it comes to inductive arguments, many do indeed move from specific to general as discussed, but there are many others which remain on the level of the specific, e.g.:

> Socrates was a philosopher and was intelligent.
> Plato was a philosopher and was intelligent.
> Bertrand Russell was a philosopher and was intelligent.
> Jean-Paul Sartre was a philosopher.
> Therefore, Jean-Paul Sartre was probably intelligent.[3]

Further, there are many inductive arguments which remain entirely on the level of the general, e.g.:

> All ancient Greek philosophers were intelligent.
> All medieval philosophers were intelligent.
> All twentieth-century philosophers are intelligent.
> Therefore, all philosophers are probably intelligent.

---

[3] To be fair, we should note that between the fourth premiss and the conclusion there is an implied general statement, i.e., All philosophers are intelligent. But this is not, and need not be, actually stated as part of the argument.

So the rather simplistic distinction between deductive and inductive arguments which deals with whether they move from general to specific (deductive) or specific to general (inductive) simply does not cover all the cases, and of course any definition which fails to be true of every case of the thing it defines is not satisfactory.

But there is a further problem with the definition we are considering. Even if it did cover every single case, it would still be a poor definition, because it does not tell us the main, or essential, difference between the two kinds of arguments. To see why this is a problem, consider this famous example: Let us say we define a human as a "featherless biped." This definition does cover all the cases. It enables us to distinguish humans from all other animals. First, we are bipeds since we walk on two feet. Second, unlike other bipeds such as chickens, we are featherless. What is wrong with the definition? Simply that, while it would enable one to identify a human, it doesn't tell what, in essence, humans are. Aristotle (384–322 B.C.) offers a much better definition: Humans are "rational animals." We are demonstrably animals from a biological standpoint, but we are rational, unlike any other animals so far as we can tell. Similarly, even if all deductive arguments did move from general to particular and all inductive arguments did move from particular to general, the **essential difference** between the two kinds of arguments is something quite different. So what is it?

The key to understanding the difference between induction and deduction comes down to what each kind of argument claims to be doing. Inductive and deductive arguments claim different things for their conclusions. Specifically, inductive arguments claim that their conclusions are only **probable,** given their premises, while deductive arguments claim that their conclusions are **necessary,** given their premises.

Let us examine this distinction in more detail. Consider the typical inductive argument we discussed above: a list of humans who are all mortal (as shown by the fact that they all have died), leading to the conclusion that all humans (including those of us now alive and those yet to be born) are mortal. The conclusion, quite clearly, "goes beyond" the premises; it encompasses more information than do the premises. Further, the conclusion might be false even if all the premises are true (the biological "laws" governing aging and death are, after all, simply descriptions of what has been observed up to now), but the probability or likelihood is overwhelmingly in favor of the conclusion being true. This inductive argument is a strong one, since as best we can tell there are no humans in the world as much as 150 years old, and very few over 100 years old. Nothing about this fact guarantees, logically, that all those humans now alive will eventually die—this conclusion could be false— but a very good case is made that they will.

Contrast this inductive argument to our classic deductive one: All humans are mortal, Socrates is human, therefore Socrates is mortal. Note first that the conclusion this time does not "go beyond" the premises: Given the truth of the premises, the conclusion must necessarily follow. This is because the conclusion simply spells out or "analyzes" (as many twentieth-century philosophers would say) what is already contained in the premisses. To say it another way, the conclusion could not possibly be false if both premisses are true, any more than a square could not fail to have four sides and still be a square.

Let us summarize these essential differences between inductive and deductive arguments. Inductive arguments:

1. Claim that their conclusions are probably true, given that the premisses are true.
2. Have conclusions which "go beyond" the premisses.
3. Have conclusions which might be false even if all of the premisses are true.

On the other hand, deductive arguments:

1. Claim that their conclusions are necessarily true, given that the premisses are true.
2. Have conclusions which do not "go beyond" the premisses.
3. Have conclusions which cannot possibly be false if all of their premisses are true.

1.5 Induction

Since the great majority of our emphasis from this point on will be on deductive arguments, we would do well to have one last look at induction. Consider the following example of a typical piece of inductive reasoning. One day someone brings a large bag of marbles into the classroom and announces that there are 1000 marbles in the bag. The members of the class are asked to decide what color the marbles are. Before the bag is opened, people might venture a guess. The marbles might be all red, or all green, or a mixture of red, white and blue, or whatever. The appropriate word here is "guess," because without any clue at all, there is no evidence on which to base the guess. No inductive argument is present without some evidence. One does not, in other words, draw a conclusion where there are no premisses. Now let us say one of the marbles is taken out of the bag and shown to everyone, and it is red. Someone says, "Oh, they're probably all red." This is an example of the weakest possible inductive argument. It is an argument, since there is a piece of evidence or a premiss. But it is a very poor argument (it "jumps to a conclusion"), since there is only the slightest reason to think that all the marbles might be red just because one is red.

Now let us say that we continue to pull marbles out of the bag, and each one in turn is observed to be red. Our inductive argument for the conclusion "They are probably all red" is getting stronger and stronger. There is no one point at which the argument moves from being poor to so-so to good; different people will feel more comfortable with the conclusion at different points. But eventually, most people would be ready to conclude that probably all the marbles are red.

Let us say that we are now at the 999th marble, and it is red. This leaves one marble left unobserved in the bag. Virtually anyone would be willing to bet that the last marble is red, too, and we now have the strongest possible inductive argument. The conclusion still goes beyond the premisses, but just barely (99.9% of the evidence is in). The argument is still inductive because it is still possible for the premisses to all be true and the conclusion false, though this possibility is so slim that we would be amazed if the last marble turned out to be a different color.

Now let us pull the last marble out of the bag and note that, sure enough, it too is red. What we now have is a report, not an inductive argument any more. We have observed 1000 marbles and each marble was red. We might even conclude, **deductively,** that therefore we have observed 1000 red marbles. We have a report, or possibly a deductive argument, but definitely not an inductive argument any more. The conclusion no longer goes beyond the premisses; it is no longer possible for the conclusion to be false if all the premisses are true. Inductive arguments, then, require something between **no evidence at all** and **complete evidence.** If we have no evidence at all our so-called "conclusion" is strictly guesswork. If we have complete evidence with nothing missing our so-called "conclusion" is simply a report. In between these extremes, when we have some evidence, we have inductive arguments of varying strength.

What does determine the strength of an inductive argument? Let us return to the example of the marbles for our answer to this question. First, it is obvious that the number of premisses we have is relevant to the strength of the argument. The more red marbles we take out of the bag, the stronger is our conclusion that they are all red. If the bag contained half red and half white marbles, then the more we took out of the bag, the closer we would get to a 50–50 ratio (though, of course, the first several could all be of one color; consider the possibilities when we flip a coin repeatedly). But just as important as the number of premisses is the representative nature of these premisses. How typical are the premisses of the whole? In the marble case, have we taken a variety of marbles out of the bag? Have we reached down deep, felt around the sides, etc., or did we remove the marbles one by one from the top? It is always possible that the bag could contain several hundred marbles of a different color which were packed in before the red ones.

When assessing the strength of inductive arguments, variety of the premisses is an important consideration. Consider a typical inductive argument: the taking of a poll. A fraction of the total population is interviewed about an issue and their views recorded. From this an inductive argument is constructed and a conclusion drawn about the population as a whole. Obviously the number of people interviewed, even in the most extensive polls, cannot begin to approach the size of the whole population. What is done, then, is to work hard to be sure that those interviewed, though relatively few in number, are representative of the variety of people in the whole population. The economic, religious, racial, cultural, age, and other differences in the population as a whole must be represented in approximately the same proportion in our polled group. The science of poll-taking has honed this to a fine skill in the past several years. We have come a long way since 1936 when a reputable magazine predicted that Alf Landon would defeat Franklin Roosevelt for the presidency based on a telephone poll! (Those with telephones in 1936 were a rather elite group, not typical of the population as a whole.) Where a large number of premises cannot be obtained, a carefully-selected variety of representative premises can strengthen an inductive argument. Conversely, where variety is not possible for some reason, a larger number is needed to produce a strong argument. Imagine that, in the marble example, the marbles are in a long tube such that they can be drawn out only in a certain order. Since we cannot "sample" the whole in this case, we would want to see a much larger number of marbles before drawing any conclusion.

A final factor in assessing the strength of an inductive argument, implied but not actually stated in what we have said so far, is the question of **how far** beyond the premises the conclusion goes. The conclusion of any inductive argument must go beyond the premises by definition, but how far it goes clearly affects the strength of the argument. To consider the marble case once again, let us say that we have observed 999 marbles out of 1000, and that they are all red. When we conclude that the 1000th and last marble is probably red, our conclusion only "goes beyond" the premises a little and as noted above, this is an excellent argument even though the last marble might possibly by another color. But imagine now that we have instead a million marbles, and we have found that 999 are red. To conclude that probably all the marbles are red would certainly "go beyond" the premises by so much that the argument would be a very weak one. (In fact, it would be comparable to our original argument where we concluded that all 1000 marbles were red based on seeing one marble.) The scope of the conclusion—how far it goes beyond the premises—is therefore a major factor in determining the success of an inductive argument. Other things being equal, the narrower the scope of the conclusion, the stronger the argument, and the broader the scope, the weaker the argument. By "narrow scope" we mean a conclusion which does not go very far beyond the premises, while a conclusion of "broad scope" goes far beyond the premises.

Another example would be the sort of situation most of us have faced when we drive in heavy traffic. Let us say we move to a new city and, on the first day's drive to work, we encounter major traffic jams and are late. In frustration we might say, "The traffic was terrible today so it will probably be terrible forever." Or we might be more temperate and say, "The traffic was terrible today so it will probably be terrible tomorrow too." The first argument has the broadest possible scope ("forever" is, after all, a long time!) and is a weak argument; the second has a narrow scope and is a strong and realistic argument.

Inductive arguments, in addition to being used by all of us constantly in our daily life, are employed extensively in probability theory and scientific method. It is to these areas that the reader wishing to learn more about induction should turn. For a discussion of the philosophical "problem of induction"—which comes down to saying that while we know **that** it works we have no idea **how**—Richard Swinburne's *The Justification of Induction* (Oxford, 1974) is recommended.

1.6 Deduction

Although both inductive and deductive arguments are used extensively, it is the deductive argument which usually is referred to when we call someone's reasoning "logical" or "illogical." Deductive arguments are always either logically successful or not; there is no "gray area" of probability or increasing likelihood as there is with their inductive counterparts. Logically successful deductive arguments are called "valid" while logically unsuccessful ones are called "invalid." Let us look, then at what makes a deductive argument (for the purposes of this discussion, we will just say "an argument") valid or invalid.

Consider this argument:

> All collies are dogs.
> All dogs are animals.
> Therefore all collies are animals.

One does not need formal instruction in logic to notice that this argument is valid. Most people can see **that** it is valid though they may not be able to say **why** it is valid. To see why, **let us first define a valid argument as an argument which has a form such that, if all of its premises are true, then its conclusion must necessarily be true.** Notice that this definition does not say that the premises of a valid argument must actually be true, nor that the conclusion must be true. It just says that if all the premises are true, then the conclusion must be true. In the argument above, it is reasonably clear that the premises and conclusion are both true, but this is not what makes the argument valid. It is the form (or structure, or pattern, or arrangement of the terms in the argument) which makes it valid. To see in a general way what the form of this argument is, let us remove the content words and substitute letters X, Y, and Z for them (X for collies, Y for dogs, and Z for animals):

> All X are Y.
> All Y are Z.
> Therefore, all X are Z.

We now have the form of the valid argument above; it is one of many valid argument forms. What it says is that for **any** X, Y, or Z, **if** all X are Y and all Y are Z, **then** all X must necessarily be Z. It is not possible, in other words, for both premisses to be true and the conclusion false. Now, depending upon what words we substitute for X, Y, and Z, we might have an argument like the above where everything is true, or one in which everything is false (try dogs, cats, and birds for X, Y, and Z!), or one in which the premisses are false and the conclusion true (dogs, cats, and canines will do it), or any of several other combinations. What we won't be able to produce with this form, however, is any X, Y and Z such that the premisses will both be true and the conclusion false. Try it! This is what the form, being valid, is a guarantee against: it guarantees us that if our premisses are both true, then necessarily the conclusion will be true. Validity is a guarantee, not of the absolute truth of the conclusion, but at least of the truth of any conclusion which follows validly from premisses which are known to be all true.

If we think of validity as like a guarantee, then an invalid argument lacks that guarantee. Specifically, invalid arguments do not have a form that guarantees us that if the premisses are all true then the conclusion will be true. This can be said in a more concise way if we simply **define an invalid argument as an argument with a form such that it is possible for all of its premisses to be true and its conclusion false.** This means that in an invalid argument, all manner of combinations of true and false premisses and conclusion will be possible (just like in a valid argument), but unlike a valid argument, the possibility of all true premisses with a false conclusion will always be there. Let us look at an invalid argument and then display its form as we did above:

> All dogs are animals.
> All cats are animals.
> Therefore, all cats are dogs.

It is clear from the definition that this argument is invalid because its premisses are clearly true and its conclusion definitely false. But what makes this argument invalid is not the fact that this actually happens, but rather that it is even **possible** for it to happen. Consider the form of this argument (X, Y, and Z this time for dogs, animals, and cats):

> All X are Y.
> All Z are Y.
> Therefore, All Z are X.

This is an invalid form because there are many X's, Y's and Z's that would give it true premisses and a false conclusion; the one above is but one example. Of course, this invalid form also allows for possible X's, Y's, and Z's that would make everything true (try dogs, animals, and collies), everything false (dogs, birds, monkeys), and all sorts of other combinations. What is important in distinguishing valid from invalid argument forms (and keep in mind that the examples above are but one example of each) is not that both will allow for a great variety of combinations of true and false premises and conclusions, but that only an invalid form will allow a combination of all true premises and false conclusion. If this combination is possible in an argument form, then that form is invalid. At this point the way to see whether a form is a valid or invalid one is to try combinations as we did above. A valid form will never allow any content (X's, Y's, and Z's) which will make all the premises true and the conclusion false; an invalid form will allow such a combination.

There are several problems, however, with the method we just used to distinguish valid from invalid argument forms. First, it relies on how imaginative we can be; a form might be invalid yet we might not be able to dream up a content which would show that. By the same token, a form might be valid and we could still wonder whether some content we hadn't yet thought of would produce all true premises and a false conclusion. Further, the variety of valid and invalid argument forms is endless; the rather straightforward arguments above are but one kind, the kind we will later call categorical syllogisms. There are many other kinds, including arguments in symbolic logic and ones for which it will not be as easy to come up with a "content" to test the validity of the form. That is why the "method" used above is only a way to illustrate the difference between valid and invalid arguments. Much of what is to follow will involve formal tests (Venn Diagrams, truth tables, rigorous proofs, and so on) which will allow us to distinguish valid from invalid arguments. It is these tests to which we referred earlier in defining logic as the "techniques" used to distinguish good from bad reasoning.

A problem remains. Look again at our example of a valid argument form:

> All X are Y.
> All Y are Z.
> Therefore, all X are Z.

Our original X, Y and Z here were collies, dogs and animals. We said the argument was valid because it is not possible for any X, Y and Z to give us both premises true and the conclusion false. We noted, though, that any other combination is possible, and that, for example, if the X, Y, and Z are dogs, cats, and birds, then both premises and the conclusion would be false. Now it is an uncomfortable thought that logic considers the following two arguments to be on an equal footing:

> All collies are dogs.
> All dogs are animals.
> Therefore, all collies are animals.

and

All dogs are cats.
All cats are birds.
Therefore, all dogs are birds.

Yet from a purely logical point of view they **are** on an equal footing. Not only are they both valid, but they are logically the same since they have the same form:

All X are Y.
All Y are Z.
Therefore, all X are Z.

We are left wondering what the good of logic is if zany arguments and perfectly sensible ones are of equal value. To address this question, we need to introduce a new term, the idea of a sound argument. **A sound argument is a valid argument in which the premises are all true.** A sound argument meets the criteria for validity, namely that if its premises are all true then its conclusion must necessarily be true. In addition, its premises **are** all true. So a sound argument must necessarily have a conclusion that is true. Our original argument, then, is sound:

All collies are dogs.
All dogs are animals.
Therefore, all collies are animals.

It is valid, for the reasons we discussed above. In addition, it is true that all collies are dogs and that all dogs are animals. The conclusion, then, is not only true, but is **proved** to be true by this argument.

On the other hand, the other argument of the same form which we were considering is valid but unsound:

All dogs are cats.
All cats are birds.
Therefore, all dogs are birds.

It is valid, because it has the same form as the valid argument above. Thus it meets the first requirement for soundness. But it is unsound because it does not meet the second requirement for soundness, namely, that all the premises be true. Both premises, in fact, are false. Thus we can indeed distinguish a reasonable from a zany argument, but notice what happened. In order to distinguish between the two, we had to leave the purely formal realm of logic and enter the "real world" of truth. From the standpoint of logic alone, as noted earlier, these two arguments are exactly the same, because they have the same form. (This is roughly equivalent to saying that two arithmetic demonstrations are the same, one in which two apples are put together with three apples to get five apples, and another in which two oranges and three oranges are put together to get five oranges. Only one arithmetic fact has been demonstrated: 2 + 3 = 5.) But logic can be applied to the real world, and when we move out of our role as logicians and into the real world where we live our lives, then we must always ask about the truth of various claims that are made. We find, of course, that some statements are clearly true and others clearly false, but that probably the vast majority of the statements offered for our consideration (and hence the arguments which these statements are frequently part of), can legitimately be debated regarding truth or falsity. Logic provides no help here in the world of content; there it is to the expert in the relevant field that we must turn.

If this seems odd, remember again our analogy of the computer. The computer will not ascertain that any information it gives you is true; only that it follows from whatever information you have fed into it. Computers, in some ways, are valid deductive logic machines; they deal with the form and not the content of our reasoning. They can be used in contexts where we try our best to make the content true (i.e. financial reports for the company), where we know that the content is false (playing games), or where we really have no idea whether the content is true or false (planning a class schedule a semester early). In all of these cases, the computer's job is not to make a judgment on the value or truth of the content it is dealing with, but to tell us what follows from the input (read "premisses") it is given.

The analogy of the computer also helps in making a final point about deduction. Granted that we want to find sound arguments in our search for truth about all sorts of things, one may still wonder why anyone would ever want to bother with arguments which are valid but unsound. Since they do not prove their conclusions to be true, what good are they? A moment's reflection about the way we actually use logic will answer this question. Sometimes, as noted above, we reason with premisses about which we do not know whether they are true or false. When a student selects courses for a future semester, it is crucial that the planning be logical. Two courses that meet at conflicting times cannot both be taken, for example. Planning in general is like that; we use deduction to show what would follow if such-and-such is the case. Often such-and-such turns out not to be the case, so both our premisses and conclusion are false. But something else, which we have also planned for, hopefully turns out to be the case; its premisses and conclusion are true. Planning is but one common activity in which valid arguments are crucial—even though many of them will turn out to be unsound due to false premisses.

Further, there are times when we reason with premisses which are known to be false. As noted above, playing a game by its rules is an example. I have never owned any ocean property, but in *Monopoly* I have often "owned" Boardwalk and have charged my tenants $2000 when they stay at my hotel there. In *Monopoly* we "plan" our capital expenditures so that we can afford to build that hotel in the first place, and in doing so we must use valid deductive arguments (e.g. if you have only $1500 in cash but $1000 in mortgage value, and if the only way to raise money immediately is to mortgage property, then it follows that if you land on my Board-walk hotel and owe me $2000, you must mortgage something).

Exercise:

I.   State in a paragraph or two the difference between inductive and deductive arguments. Comment briefly on the problems involved when one defines this difference by saying that induction moves from specific to general statements while deduction moves from general to specific statements.

II.   Answer the following questions:

1.   True or False: Deductive and inductive arguments both claim that their conclusions follow necessarily from their premisses.

2.   What determines the validity or invalidity of a deductive argument is: (a) its form; (b) its content; (c) its inductive probability.

3.   True or False: In an inductive argument, it is possible for the premisses to all be true and the conclusion false.

4.   In a valid deductive argument, if all the premisses are true, then: (a) the conclusion is probably but not necessarily true; (b) the conclusion is definitely true; (c) there is no way of telling whether the conclusion is true.

5.   True or False: It is possible for a valid deductive argument to have all false premisses and a false conclusion.

6.   True or False: It is possible for an invalid argument to have all true premisses and a true conclusion.

7.   A "sound" argument: (a) is valid and has all true premisses; (b) has all true premisses but may not be valid; (c) is valid but may not have all true premisses.

8.   When we affirm something on the basis of no evidence at all, this can best be described as: (a) a deductive argument; (b) an inductive argument; (c) a guess.

9.   True or False: In the "real world" there are never situations where we would reason with premisses known not to be true.

10. True or False: From the purely logical point of view, all valid arguments are equally "successful."

------------CHAPTER TWO------------

Everyday Mistakes in Reasoning

2.1 Logical vs. Psychological Mistakes

When we are presented with a piece of reasoning, we sometimes accept it because we see that it is "logical." This may mean, as we have already seen, that it is either **inductively** probable or likely that the conclusion is true given the premises, or **deductively** valid such that the conclusion must be true if the premises are all true. There are times, however, when we accept a piece of reasoning not so much because it seems "logical" in either of these senses, but because of some **psychological** factor which leads us to accept it. Most of this book will focus on identifying and avoiding logical mistakes in reasoning—sometimes called "formal fallacies"—but in this chapter we will concentrate on mistakes of the psychological kind, sometimes known as "informal fallacies." Informal fallacies are very common; we have all "fallen for them" at some time or other, and have most likely used them on others as well. There are many lists of informal fallacies and indeed whole books devoted to them.[1] Our purpose in this chapter is a modest one; we will look briefly at some of the more common ones, see why each is a fallacy or mistake, and offer a few suggestions on avoiding such faulty reasoning. Some of these fallacies have been given Latin names, as they have been the subject of philosophical debate for centuries.

2.2 Informal Fallacies: Some Typical Psychological Mistakes

Argumentum ad Baculum

In English, this argument is sometimes known as the "Appeal to Force." Sometimes we accept a "conclusion" because we have reason to think that something

---

[1] One of the best such books is S. Morris Engel's *With Good Reason: An Introduction to the Informal Fallacies,* published by St. Martin's Press. (New York).

unpleasant will happen to us if we do not accept it. The boss asks you to stay and work late tonight, and also mentions that it is almost time to decide who among the employees will get a raise in salary. This is not literally a threat of "force," of course, but the psychological connection between staying late and getting the raise (or between not staying late and not getting the raise) is very powerful. You "conclude" that you should stay late.

This fallacy is present whenever someone draws a conclusion based upon either an explicit or an implicit "threat" of unpleasant consequences. The threat above is implicit; the boss certainly does not **promise** to give a raise if the employee stays, or for that matter to withhold a raise if the employee does not stay. Sometimes, of course, the threat can be explicit: "Give me your candy or I'll punch you in the nose!" There is no **logical** connection here between the "premises" and the "conclusion," but psychologically we tend to associate the two—perhaps because we know from experience that often explicit or implicit "threats" are indeed carried out. The lesson here is not that we should never "give in" in such cases—simply that we should be aware of the dynamics of what we are doing and why.

Argumentum ad Hominem

Literally, "argument directed to the man," this fallacy occurs when we ignore the reasons someone gives us for the conclusion he or she wants us to accept, and direct our attention instead to the person giving the argument. We might make fun of the person (the "abusive" **ad hominem**), or we might suggest that the person's special circumstances make his or her statements incorrect or irrelevant (the "circumstantial" ad hominem). In either case, we are disregarding the **reasons** being given for the conclusion we are being asked to accept.

Consider the following examples of the "abusive" form of the **ad hominem** fallacy:

"Pay no attention to what that punk says; just look at him!"

"This witness is a known liar; obviously she is lying today."

"Those _____ never get anything straight; obviously this person's claim is false." (insert in the blank any group typically discriminated against: ethnic/racial/gender/political, etc.)

Here, on the other hand, are some examples of the "circumstantial" form:

"Of course Rev. Smith believes in God; obviously his arguments for God's existence can have no merit."

"My literature teacher thinks I should read more books; but naturally **she** would have to say that."

"Mr. Speaker, we should disregard the testimony of the CEO of Megacorp, Inc., in favor of lower corporation taxes. He is not in a position to be objective."

How do we avoid the **ad hominem** fallacy? This is easier said than done. It is easy to look at the examples above and see ourselves as "above" drawing such foolish conclusions, but the fact is that we often carry biases, prejudices, and preconceived ideas into our daily lives. We must redouble our efforts to be aware of these and avoid being taken in by them. We must, in short, neither engage in such "reasoning" nor allow ourselves to be persuaded when others do so.

Argumentum ad Ignorantiam

Psychologically, the argument "from ignorance" is a powerful one. We use it when we say that something must be so since no one has shown that it is **not** so. We also use it when we say the opposite, that something must **not** be so since no one has ever shown that it **is** so. There are numerous examples:

"Extraterrestrials obviously exist, because no one has ever proved that they do not."

"You can't prove that God exists, so God must not exist."

"No one can show that a human fetus is a person, so it must not be a person."

"No one can show that a human fetus is not a person, so it must be a person."

"You must have committed the crime since you can't prove that you didn't."

Notice that this last example is exactly the sort of faulty reasoning that our legal assumption of "innocent until proven guilty" is designed to confront. One might think at first that "innocent until proven guilty" is actually a case where **ad ignorantiam** is not a fallacy but a solid piece of reasoning. ("So-and-so is innocent since we can't prove that he is guilty.") It is more realistic, though, to look at this legal assumption as just what it is—an assumption which a jury is **required by law to make.** It is all-too-tempting to assume the opposite, "guilty until proven innocent." In order to guard against this and preserve the rights of anyone accused of a crime, we require a judge or jury to assume the person to be innocent until he or she has been proven guilty by the removal of "reasonable doubt." This important legal safeguard does not make it any less a fallacy in ordinary situations to say that something **is** so because it has not been proved **not so,** and vice-versa.

Argumentum ad Populum

This is the argument directed "to the people." There are several versions of it. It can be an appeal to what is **popular,** such as one often finds in advertisements. A certain product should be purchased because "everyone uses it," or perhaps more subtly because "everyone who's anyone uses it." Often the pitch is designed to suggest that the user of the product will acquire a certain characteristic which will make him or her popular. This might be an attractive physique, "whiter-than-white" teeth, soft wrinkle-free skin, or whatever. Peer pressure being what it is, this is a powerful psychological tool. Logically, of course, it certainly does not follow that what the majority thinks is true, **is** true just for that reason.

A slightly different version of the **ad populum** is to appeal to a **growing** popular or even patriotic sentiment in favor of a product, a political candidate, a position on a national issue, or whatever. Sometimes called the "bandwagon," effect, its appeal is hard to resist. No one wants to feel "left out," and if we can be persuaded that "more and more people are joining" the movement for whatever it is, we are seriously tempted to sign on.

A famous example of the bandwagon effect occurred at the 1960 Democratic National Convention. Sen. John F. Kennedy had been campaigning for the presidential nomination for several years by this time. The weekend before the convention began, Sen. Lyndon B. Johnson, the flamboyant and popular Senate Majority Leader, threw his hat into the ring. Television coverage of the early hours of the convention suggested a dead heat between Kennedy and Johnson, but at the end of the first day, one or two key Johnson delegates announced that they were switching their support to Kennedy. Soon television reporters were asking other delegates for their reaction to this news, and a few other delegates made the same switch. By the next day there was talk of a growing "Kennedy bandwagon," as more and more delegates signed on to what they now perceived as the winning side. This, of course, made it the winning side, and Kennedy was eventually nominated by acclamation.

Argumentum ad Misericordiam

This is the "appeal to pity" (or perhaps "misery"), and we must admit that everyone engages in it from time to time. It occurs when someone asks for a special favor or special consideration, not on the grounds that it is merited, but because of something that makes us want to pity him or her and thus offer help. Consider:

"Please accept my late assignment; I worked so hard it gave me a terrible headache."

"Please acquit this defendant; he had a miserable and deprived childhood."

"If my remarks this evening are not particularly coherent, it is because I lost my notes and will have to ad lib my talk."

"The only political gift I ever accepted from anyone was a little dog named Checkers. My kids love that dog, and we're going to keep it."

Although this last example is rather well-known, by far the most famous example of this fallacy occurs in Plato's dialogue, *The Apology*. Socrates, in defending himself against the charge that he has corrupted the youth of Athens, tells his jury that he will not bring his wife and children before the court to weep and plead for his acquittal. By mentioning that he has a family, he thus gains some sympathy from the jury which will decide his fate. In addition, he perhaps gains some admiration for being strong enough to not bring his family in to plead for him. In a sense, Socrates tries to have it both ways! (In the end, he has it **neither** way: he is found guilty and executed.)

Note that the listing of **ad Misericordiam** as an informal fallacy does not affect whatever moral, ethical, or religious obligations we might have to those whom we pity. The fallacy is simply to claim that our obligation somehow follows logically from the fact that the person is to be pitied. Not all of our most important obligations in life are necessarily rooted in logic.

Argumentum ad Verecundiam

Known as the "appeal to authority," this is the mistake we make when we accept the word of a person known as an authority or expert in **some** field, but **not** the field in which he or she is now speaking. For example, if a nuclear physicist has an opinion about economics, the fact that this individual is an expert in nuclear physics does not make the opinion in economics any more or less worth accepting. Anyone, of course, can have an opinion about economics and perhaps be correct. And on the other hand, a nuclear physicist can always engage in the study of economics and thus become something of an expert in that field. But to accept as true just any opinion—on **any** matter—of a person who is an expert on **other** matters, is to commit this fallacy. Some examples:

"Dr. Jones, our family physician, told me that our country needs to go back to the gold standard. I don't know much about these things, but I guess the doctor must be right."

"I'm anxious to hear the lecture by the famous biologist, Dr. Sally Smith. She's speaking on the need for reform in our political system."

"Joe Hunk, the popular young actor, says that Pepsi is the best soft drink, so from now on I'm drinking Pepsi."

Notice that the last example in particular is a very common one. If an advertisement simply associates its product with popularity, sex appeal, or "good times," then the fallacy of **ad Populum** is committed. But when a well-known **person** endorses a product, it is well to suspect the fallacy of **ad Verecundiam.** The broadcast and print media are full of endorsements in which actors, politicians, and other well-known people assure us that certain products are the best of their kind. Now of course, it is not always a fallacy to give credit to such endorsements. An endorsement of a certain brand of basketball shoe by a famous basketball player—especially when that player can be seen wearing those shoes in games—is certainly more impressive than the same player endorsing a certain brand of soft drink. Why? Because a basketball player can reasonably be assumed to have some expertise in the performance of basketball shoes. On the other hand, we all have different tastes in soft drinks, and the tastes of a famous basketball player may or may not be the same as ours.

Sometimes this fallacy is committed in a more subtle way. Often we take the testimony of an expert who **is** speaking in his or her area of expertise, and we simply misunderstand or take out of context what was being said. A famous example is the notion held by many that Albert Einstein endorsed an ethical position called "relativism." Relativism is the view that there are no absolute or ultimate values or ethical standards, and that what is right or wrong is thus **relative** to what a person, or a culture, or an historical era, says it is. Einstein, of course, is best known for the General and Special Theories of Relativity in physics. In the very limited context of his discussions of space and time Einstein did say, in effect, that "everything is relative." This is often taken, out of context, to mean that **everything** is relative, including values and moral standards. Such a conclusion would commit the fallacy of **Argumentum ad Verecundiam.**

When considering the opinions of experts, we need first to ask ourselves whether this person is an expert in the subject about which he or she is now speaking. Second, we need to ask whether we have correctly understood the meaning of what was said and the context in which it was said. Once we have considered these matters, then an expert's testimony can be treated, not necessarily as proof, but as important information which should at least be taken into account.

Post Hoc Ergo Propter Hoc

Literally, "after the thing, therefore because of the thing," this fallacy is usually referred to as **post hoc** or simply as "false cause." Philosophically it is a very good question just what constitutes a cause, but it is generally agreed that **one** requirement to call something X the cause of something else Y is that X must **precede** Y in time. If we say that the window broke because a baseball flew through it, then the baseball must first have been moving toward the window. The fallacy of false cause occurs when we assume that **just because** something X preceded something else Y, then X must have caused Y. A little thought will show that this is not always the case. The playing of the National Anthem precedes most sports events, but does not **cause** the events to be played. Some children who play with toy cars are in car accidents later when they are teenagers, but this does not mean one **causes** the other. Whatever a "true cause" is, more is required than merely that it precede its effect. Further, not all events that precede other events are the cause of the latter events.

A humorous example of the fallacy occurs in Mark Twain's *A Connecticut Yankee in King Arthur's Court*. Hank Morgan, the American factory worker who is magically transported through time to King Arthur's court, is about to be burned at the stake. Just as the fire is to be lit, he remembers that on this particular date in history, an eclipse of the sun occurred at exactly this hour. He tells the King and court that if they harm him, he will blot out the sun and they will all perish. The king's men hurry to light the fire before Hank can carry out his threat. Just then someone notices a slight darkening in the sky, and Hank dramatically points to the sun. The people are terrified and the king begs Hank to allow the sun to shine again. Since he cannot remember how long an eclipse lasts, Hank tells them he must let the sun be blotted out for awhile to teach them all a lesson. Finally, with a promise from the king to make Hank a major player in the administration of the kingdom, he "allows" the sun to return. The king and the people of Camelot are convinced that Hank "caused" the eclipse to both begin and end.

More serious examples of the fallacy are found when we notice trends and correlations and infer cause-effect relationships from them. For example:

> "In the years since MTV has been on cable television, drug use has tripled. Need we say more?"

> "We built up our military in the early eighties, and the Berlin Wall came down in the late eighties. It was a good investment."

> "The divorce rate has increased at the same pace as the rate of juvenile crimes. Clearly there is a connection."

The reason these are important examples is that, while the correlations referred to do not necessarily mean that the first event in each is the cause of the second, it might well be that there **is** a cause-effect relationship in one or more of these cases. Cause-effect relationships require serious study, and while the cause must precede the effect, there is much more we must look for as well. As they stand above, with no further information, each of the above examples definitely commits the fallacy of false cause.

Black or White Fallacy

Also known as the "either-or" or "false dichotomy" fallacy, this is a typical mistake made by most of us from time to time. It is a failure to see that there are alternatives between two extremes:

"I have to pass this test or I'll flunk out of college."

"You must marry me or I'll be miserable and die."

"America: Love It or Leave It" (a common slogan during the Vietnam War)

"Either you love him or you hate him."

As we shall see later in this book, there are some "either-or" statements which **are** mutually exclusive of each other, such as "Either I will be married or I will not be married." There are no other alternatives here, assuming that the terms are carefully defined. But the examples above and many other similar ones are not like this. There are alternatives between the extremes in each case. I might not pass the test and yet be granted an opportunity to stay in college. You might not marry me and I might get over it, etc. Circumstances sometimes make it very difficult to see the reasonable alternatives involved in a situation; here is where statements like the above examples might be made and where the "Black or White" fallacy is committed. It is so named because we often accuse people who regularly "reason" this way as thinking in "black and white" terms—as if there were no colors other than black and white.

Petitio Principii

Also known as "begging the question," this fallacy is somewhat odd because, unlike the others discussed so far, it **is** logically valid. Yet it is a fallacy: let's see why. It occurs when we argue for a conclusion by giving as our premises statements which simply restate the conclusion in a different way. Thus, "You should study logic because you ought to learn the techniques of correct reasoning," begs the question. We defined logic as the study of the techniques used to distinguish correct from incorrect reasoning, so the above really says that you ought to study logic because you ought to study logic. Now this **is** a valid argument: there is no way the premiss could ever be true and the conclusion false (since they basically say the same thing). But it is still a fallacy if it is taken as providing a **reason** for studying logic. It is, in other words, a fallacy to think that this "argument" provides anything other than a single statement made twice in slightly different ways. It's "form" could be stated as "L, therefore L," where L stands for "You ought to study logic." This comes down to nothing more than saying that if L is true, then L is true.

Sometimes this fallacy is also known as "circular reasoning" or "arguing in a circle." A standard example illustrating this circularity is the following: "What the Bible says is true because it is inspired by God. And we know that there is a God because the Bible says so." Using the letters "B" and "G," we could express this as: "B because G, and G because B." As long as one assumes **either** that God exists **or** that what the Bible says is true, then one can prove the other statement. The problem is that we cannot prove one of these **unless** we assume the other. (This does not rule out religious faith, of course, since this is usually held to be something different from logical proof. It also does not rule out **other** attempts to logically prove either that the Bible is true or that God exists.)

Complex Question

This fallacy is closely related to the one above; it also involves a form of begging the question. Consider a question which already "builds in" an assumption, such as: "Why did you rob that bank?" "Are you embarrassed about being late?" "When will you get a job?" etc. These questions assume, in turn, that you did rob that bank, you were late, and you will get a job. Now if these assumptions are shared by all concerned, there is no fallacy. If, for example, you have admitted that you robbed the bank, then the question of why you did it might be appropriate. The fallacy of complex question occurs when the assumption built into the question is not shared by all concerned. The question is designed to force an admission that the assumption is true. Consider:

> A. Why did you rob that bank?
> B. I—uh—don't know . . .
> A. So you admit that you did rob the bank!

When B. says that he "doesn't know," this is taken to mean that he doesn't know **why he robbed the bank,** thus admitting that he did rob it. The question was designed to produce this kind of response, even though B. might have meant only that he "doesn't know" what to say in response to such a question. A more proper response to a complex question is the following:

> A. Are you embarrassed about being late?
> B. You're asking me two things. First, I was not late; I was in the back room filing some things when you arrived. Second, I **am** embarrassed, but it's because you are making such an issue of this!

Accident and Converse Accident

Both of these fallacies concern the relationship between general statements and particular cases which may seem to apply to them. The fallacy of accident occurs when one uses the general statement as a premiss, and then concludes that the particular case is a specific application of that general statement. Sometimes, of course, we do this quite legitimately and commit no fallacy, as in the following example:

"Stealing is wrong; therefore you shouldn't steal."

Because of such obvious cases, we are sometimes tempted to think that just **any** specific example, no matter how its "accidental" circumstances may make it unusual, must apply to the general case of which it is an example. Consider this situation, paraphrased from Plato's **Republic:**

> "It is right to return someone's property to him when he asks for it.
> Thus, if a friend asks you to keep his weapon and then returns, angry
> and drunk, and asks for it with the clear intention of harming someone,
> it is right to give it back to him."

Even though this is a case of "returning someone's property to him when he asks for it," it is sufficiently unusual to make it an exception to the general rule. Indeed, our moral hunches suggest that it would be quite wrong to return the weapon to the friend in this circumstance. Consider the slogan, "Friends Don't Let Friends Drive Drunk," which suggests that we should not give a friend his own car keys if he is drunk. To ignore the unusual cases and blindly apply a rule to **each and every** situation which can be said to fall under it, is to risk committing the fallacy of accident.

The fallacy of "converse accident" is the opposite situation, and indeed is also known as the fallacy of "hasty generalization." Sometimes we consider an unusual situation and generalize that what applies to it must apply to all similar cases. Consider the reverse of Plato's case:

> "It is right to refuse to give a drunk friend his weapon when he asks for
> it. Therefore it is right to refuse to return anyone's property when asked
> to do so."

Often we are all too willing to "jump to conclusions." Consider the prohibitionists, who were convinced that alcohol should be illegal for all since it clearly cannot be handled safely by some people. On the other side, consider the argument advanced by many that marijuana should be legalized for all since it has some beneficial effects, such as in the treatment of certain eye diseases.

In assessing arguments which involve specific cases and general statements, it is important to ask whether the specific case is sufficiently **unusual** or **atypical** as to make the argument suspect. Looking at the examples above, we might ask whether treatment of eye diseases is a typical use of marijuana, whether people who cannot handle alcohol safely are typical drinkers of alcohol, whether people who ask for their property back are typically drunk and angry, etc. In this way, we have a better chance of avoiding the fallacies of both accident and converse accident.

Division and Composition

These fallacies are somewhat similar to accident and converse accident. The former fallacies, as we have just seen, occur where we deal with the relationship between general statements and unusual cases. Division and Composition deal rather with **wholes** and **parts.** Consider an entire automobile as contrasted with every part of that automobile. Some characteristics will be the same for the whole and the parts, e.g., the whole automobile is a Chevy and every part is a Chevy part (one wonders whether this is ever true in fact, but let's assume it for the sake of the example!). But other characteristics of wholes and parts are different, e.g. the whole car is very expensive but not every individual part is very expensive. The fallacy of division occurs when we say that just any characteristic of a whole thing is also a characteristic of each part of a thing. Composition is the opposite, when we say that the characteristics of the parts of a thing must also be the characteristics of the whole. Here are some examples of both fallacies:

> NBC is a major television network, so the NBC representative who spoke to our class today must be a key person in the television business.—*Division*

> Each of these books is very light and easy to carry, so it will be an easy job to transfer all the books in this room to the next room. —*Composition*

> Every member of the NBA All-Star Team is one of the best players in professional basketball, so the All-Star Team must be the best team in professional basketball.—*Composition*

> *The Sound of Music* is one of the greatest musicals of all time, so every song in it must be among the greatest songs of all time.—*Division*

These examples all refer to whole **things** (a television network, a room full of books, a basketball team, a Broadway musical), and individual **parts** of those things (an employee of the network, an individual book, a member of the team, a song from the musical). A slightly different form of the fallacies of division and composition can occur when we take a term such as "students," and use it to refer both to individual students and to students in general. When we say, "The students are talking with the professor at his desk," we are referring to certain individual students; this is sometimes called the "distributive" use of the term. But when we say, "The students at my college come from all 50 states and 20 foreign countries," we obviously are referring to the student body as a **whole;** this is sometimes called the "collective" use of the term. Neither of these statements by itself commits a fallacy, of course, but consider the following: "The students at my college come from all 50 states and 20 foreign countries, so my student friend Jane Doe must come from all 50 states and 20 foreign countries." This would be a version of the fallacy of division, one in which the collective and distributive senses of the term are confused. A similar example which would commit the fallacy of composition would be the following: "The Metro subway train I ride to work each day carries many more passengers than any automobile on the road. Therefore, Metro subway trains carry more passengers to work each day than automobiles do."

Equivocation

Many words have more than one meaning. Normally, when we use these terms the context makes our meaning clear. Thus, when we say, "It is my right to refuse to speak to you," it is understood that the word "right" is used to refer to one's political freedom of action. But consider the question, "Is it right to refuse to speak to someone?" Here the word "right" has a moral sense: is it **morally** correct to refuse to speak to someone? Both of these cases are clear individually, but consider the following "argument": "It is my right to refuse to speak with you, so it must be right for me to do so." This commits the fallacy of equivocation, or as we normally say, it "equivocates on the word 'right'." Equivocation is very common with moral terms such as "good," "bad," "right," and "wrong." A person who makes a bad decision, for example, is not necessarily a bad person, but consider how often we "reason" in this way. Equivocation can also occur with terms which get their meaning in relation to something else. For instance, the term "heavy" means something quite different when it is followed by "child" then when it is followed by "horse." The heaviest child would still not weigh as much as a normal-sized horse.

A wonderful example of equivocation occurs in Homer's **Odyssey.** Odysseus, on his journey home from the Trojan War, is captured by the one-eyed Cyclops who threatens to eat him and his men. Odysseus tells the Cyclops that his name is "Nobody," and proceeds to ply the monster with wine until he falls asleep. Quickly, Odysseus takes a red-hot poker and puts out the Cyclops' eye. When the Cyclops comes raging out of his cave, his friends ask who blinded him. "Nobody did this to me!" he roars, whereupon his friends return to their homes. Fortunately for literary history, Odysseus and his men then make their escape.

Amphiboly

This fallacy is similar to equivocation, but here the "double meaning" turns not on an individual word which has more than one sense, but rather on a whole phrase or expression which can be taken in more than one way. Consider something as simple as "John said Mary come here," where the absence of adequate punctuation makes it unclear whether John is asking Mary to come here or vice-versa. The fallacy of amphiboly would occur if the statement had been intended one way but was then taken in the other way. This frequently happens in written communication due to grammatical or sentence construction problems.

Sometimes a statement can be taken in more than two ways. Consider this example: "The shooting of the cowboys is awful." This could mean any of the following:

1. It is awful that the cowboys have been shot.
2. The cowboys are awful shooters; their shots always miss.
3. The film we shot of the cowboys is awful; it will have to be retaken.

The third of these could also be viewed, perhaps, as an equivocation on "shoot"; this example shows how closely equivocation and amphiboly are related. In any case, if someone says "The shooting of the cowboys is awful" and means #1, but someone who hears this takes it as meaning #2, the fallacy of amphiboly has been committed.

2.3 How Can Mistakes in Reasoning be Avoided?

To avoid being taken in by these and the many other informal fallacies which exist, the following questions can be helpful. Some of them will remind you of specific fallacies; others are more general cautions. They should be asked whenever an argument is being considered.

1. What, if anything, is being assumed, either by the arguer or by the person considering the merits of the argument?

2. Are the terms clearly defined? Is their meaning the same each time they appear?

3. Are different phrases or expressions which mean the same thing being used?

4. Are any cause-effect relationships being assumed?

5. Are any authorities cited? If so, are they authorities in the subject area in which they are being cited? Are they being cited accurately, and in context?

6. Is anyone's opinion being ruled in—or out—because of something about that **person** which is irrelevant to the argument?

7. Is there any real or implied consequence—pleasant or unpleasant—of accepting the conclusion?

8. Does the argument rely on something having **not** been proved, or does it try positively to prove something?

9. Is it being suggested or implied that the conclusion should be accepted out of pity or compassion?

10. Are there alternatives to the conclusion which have not been explored?

11. Does the argument deal with general statements in relation to unusual or atypical cases which seem to be examples of them?

12. Does the argument discuss attributes of whole things and the parts of these things?

Once these and similar questions are asked and reflected upon, the chances of being fooled by an informal fallacy will be greatly diminished. This, however, is where the real work begins. The rest of this book will be concerned with formal reasoning and how we may identify and avoid mistakes here. This is the main business of the study of logic.

Exercises:

I.   Each of the examples below clearly commits one of the informal fallacies just discussed. Identify which one it is. Each of the fallacies occurs at least once.

1. I'm right because I'm in charge of this project, and the reason I'm in charge of this project is that I'm right!

2. My physics professor is a Democrat, and if a Ph.D. scientist is a Democrat I guess I should be one too.

3. Mr. Jones must be a very important man, because he works for General Motors and it's one of the most important corporations in the world.

4. I don't like the looks of that young man and the way he dresses. Don't pay any attention to anything he says.

5. I know John said Sally sit down.

6. Please acquit my client, your honor. He cannot afford a fine and he needs to return to work to support his family.

7. Boss: I hope you can work late tonight. By the way, I'll be making decisions about possible layoffs within the next few days.

8. I hear the president of one of the big medical insurance companies is testifying to Congress about health care reform. I guess we all know what **he'll** say.

9. I've heard of cases where people in traffic accidents have actually been held in their cars and been injured because they were wearing safety belts. Obviously it's a bad idea to wear those things!

10. Be sure to get a case of Blotto Beer for the party. That's the one in all those commercials showing great parties!

11. You'll never convince me that there's no such thing as ESP; I've never seen anyone disprove it.

12. Why are you surprised that Jill fell and broke her leg this afternoon? I saw her walk under a ladder this morning.

13. Of course you should turn right at the next intersection. What would you rather do—turn wrong?

14. Look at all the great players they selected to this year's All-Star Team. What a great team it's gonna be!

15. I know you're in pain, and I wish I could drive faster to get you to the hospital. But the speed limit here is 35 mph.

16. Hey, we can drive as fast as we want anytime. Why, just last week my friend got off without a ticket when he was rushing his wife to the hospital at 80 mph.

17. Statistics show that children who watch more than 4 hours of TV a day have trouble concentrating in school. Need we say more?

18. I'm feeling really pressured about this interview today. Either I get the job and eventually become president of the company, or I'll never get a job in my life!

19. I think I blew the interview. Why am I always so stupid?

20. From now on I'm buying nothing but Sludge Soda. That's the kind my favorite movie star drinks—it says so right in this ad.

21. "**Do,** a deer, a female deer; **Re,** a drop of golden sun . . ." (Do, Re, Mi, from *The Sound of Music*)

22. We should all support this bill. It's on the side of the flag and all that has made our nation great.

23. Why is my opponent lying? What is he hiding?

24. My friend did **not** commit the crime. She's never given me any reason to think that she would do such a thing.

25. That guy over there committed the crime, all right. He can't prove he was out of town that day, can he?

II.   Now make up or find some fallacies of your own. Try to find at least one example of each one we have discussed. Can you find any examples where **more** than one fallacy is committed?

CHAPTER THREE

Classical Logic

3.1 Aristotle and His Importance

To say that the formal study of logic is indebted to Aristotle, or even to call Aristotle the "father of logic," is still to understate the role of the great Greek thinker. Aristotle (384–322 B.C.) was not only master of every field of learning which existed in his day, he was the inventor of many of them. What we take for granted as the method of science—observation, hypothesis, experiment, etc.—we owe to Aristotle. Not only the method but also the content of the science of biology is from him in its original state; he classified living things into similar types and dissected eggs to observe the embryonic development of chicks. He wrote the first book on physics (*physis* = nature); in it he discussed motion and change. Aside from science, Aristotle wrote on psychology, on ethics and the good life (his *Nichomachean Ethics* is one of the great classics in this field), and on politics (*polis* = city-state). In this latter area he wrote both theoretical works on the ideal society and very practical descriptions of the actual political institutions of his day. His book on literary criticism, the *Poetics,* with its descriptions of the formula for a successful tragedy (protagonist, tragic flaw, etc.), has been used by playwrights and literature scholars for over 2,000 years. In pure philosophy and in theology, Aristotle constructed a system which has challenged and inspired students in these fields ever since his time, and which provided the major philosophical influence behind Thomas Aquinas' seminal work, *Summa Theologica.* Aquinas, himself the intellectual giant of a scholarly age, meticulously quotes from and cites his many predecessors by name—but when the reference is to Aristotle, the title used is simply "The Philosopher."

Aristotle's writings in logic, then, are but one facet of a many-faceted thinker's work. It would, of course, be incorrect to say that he was the first person to **be** logical, but he was the first person to seriously examine the question of what it **means** to be logical. He wanted to know what makes human reasoning work—how we can distinguish between correct and incorrect reasoning so that we can practice the correct and avoid the incorrect kind. This we recognize as the business of logic as stated in the first chapter of this book. In what follows we will consider basically the questions Aristotle asked and the answers he gave, but in a contemporary way. The following is not intended, in other words, to give an account of Aristotle's logic as Aristotle himself presented it (many such accounts can be found in various histories of philosophy, or in the original works of Aristotle such as the *Categories, De Interpretatione,* and especially the *Prior Analytics* and *Posterior Analytics*). Rather, we will discuss the concepts of the categorical proposition and categorical syllogism—Aristotle's concepts—in a way which will help us to determine the correctness of reasoning—Aristotle's goal—but we will do so using contemporary language and examples.

3.2 Classes and Categorical Propositions

Much, though not all, of the content of our everyday reasoning has to do with how classes or groups of things relate to each other. Classes are simply groups or collections of things which have in common some quality or characteristic which we mention. Some examples of classes would be: dogs, brown dogs, brown things, dogs in my yard today, unicorns, stars in the sky, books I am reading at this moment, etc. Notice how varied classes can be! They can be very large groups with an almost indefinite number of members (stars in the sky), they can have just one member (books I am reading at this moment), or they can have no members at all (unicorns). In describing a class we have to be very specific, and we have to use nouns or noun phrases. For example, "in my yard" is not a class, but "things in my yard" is. "Run" is not a class but "runners" is.

When we talk about how classes relate to each other we make statements which are known as **categorical propositions.** (Recall that, throughout this book, the words "statement" and "proposition" are used synonymously.) The recipe for a "standard form" categorical proposition is as follows: First, we must talk about two classes; typically we designate them "S" and "P" for subject and predicate class respectively. Second, we must say whether S is **included in** P or **excluded from** P, and finally, we must say to what extent this inclusion or exclusion occurs. We relate S to P using some form of the verb "to be": is, are, was, were, will be, will not be (the tense is unimportant). The verb of the categorical proposition is known as the "copula." Specifically, the following four things can be said:

> All S are P.
> No S are P.
> Some S are P.
> Some S are not P.

Consider each of the categorical propositions in turn. When we say "All S are P," we are saying that the entire class of S is included in P. We are making a **universal** statement about every member of S, and we are **affirming** that every member of S is included in P. This first proposition, then, is known as the **universal affirmative** proposition. The S and P can stand for any classes at all, of course, so any categorical proposition can be either true or false. A true example of a universal affirmative proposition would be "All dogs are animals."

The second categorical proposition, "No S are P," also makes a statement about the entire class of S, but this time the statement says that every member of S is excluded from the class of P. "No dogs are cats" would be an example of a true proposition of this kind. It is obvious why this is called the **universal negative** proposition.

In the third and fourth propositions, we are no longer dealing with every member of the S class but only with certain members of S. For our purposes, the word "some" will mean "at least one." So "Some S are P" says that there is at least one member of S which is included in the class of P. This proposition deals with a **particular** member (or members) of S, and affirms something about that member (or members), so it is known as the **particular affirmative** proposition. "Some dogs are brown things" is a true example of such a proposition.

In the fourth proposition, "Some S are not P," we are saying that at least one member of S is **excluded** from P, so this is known as the **particular negative** proposition. "Some dogs are not brown things" would be a true example here.

The four propositions are often designated by capital letters for convenience; the Latin words "AFFIRMO" and "NEGO" ("I affirm" and "I deny" respectively) may be the source of these letters. The first vowel of each word designates the two universal propositions of each kind, with the second vowel designating the two particular ones:

A = universal affirmative, "All S are P"
E = universal negative, "No S are P"
I = particular affirmative, "Some S are P"
O = particular negative, "Some S are not P"

Each of the categorical propositions has a "quantity" and a "quality." The quantity of the proposition is simply the number of members of the subject class to which the proposition refers. There are only two quantities, universal and particular. The A and E propositions are universal because they make statements about **every** member of the subject class; the I and O propositions are particular because they make statements only about **some** members of the subject class. The first word of each categorical proposition is its "quantifier," or word which indicates the quantity. "All" and "No" are the two universal quantifiers and "Some" is the particular quantifier.

The quality of the proposition is always either affirmative or negative. Members of S are either included in P or excluded from P. Thus the A and I propositions are affirmative in quality while the E and O propositions are negative in quality. Each of the categorical propositions listed above, then, has its own unique combination of quantity and quality.

We are now in a position to describe the general pattern of any categorical proposition. We begin with a quantifier ("all" or "no" if universal, "some" if particular), followed by the subject term, the copula, and the predicate term:

Quantifier—Subject Term—Copula—Predicate Term

One further point to note about the categorical propositions has to do with whether they do or do not "distribute" their class terms. Consider what it means to distribute anything at all. If a teacher distributes exams to a class, he or she must make sure that each member of the class has one. Someone who is hired to distribute advertising leaflets in a neighborhood must leave one at each house. Similarly, if we distribute a class term (S or P) in a categorical proposition, we must be sure that every member of that class is "covered." We must **say something about** each member of S or P to have distributed that term. Now, consider the four categorical propositions in turn:

All S are P: Clearly we distribute the subject term here; we use the universal quantifier "All" and we thus say something about every member of S. We say, specifically, that every member of S is included in P. We do not, however, distribute the predicate term. "All dogs are animals" says nothing about what other animals may exist. "All S are P" leaves wide open the question of whether there are any members of P beyond those which are S.

No S are P: Here we distribute both the subject and the predicate terms. Every member of S is excluded from P, so every member of P must also be excluded from S. "No dogs are cats" tells us something about every dog (it is not a cat) and also something about every cat (it is not a dog).

Some S are P: Since the particular affirmative proposition says that at least one member of S is also a member of P, it does not distribute either term. It makes no claim about every member of S but only about certain (one or more) members of S. It says of these certain members of S that they are members of P, and this certainly does not give us information about every member of P either. "Some dogs are brown things," merely says that there is at least one object in the world which is both a dog and a brown thing; it says nothing about the other members—if any—of either class.

Some S are not P: The subject of the O proposition is undistributed for the same reason that the subject of the I proposition is undistributed. When we say "Some S" we are obviously not referring to every member of S. But the predicate of the O proposition is another matter. It **is** distributed, and to see why, let us imagine a situation in which an

O proposition might be used. At the college where I teach, a preliminary computer-generated class list is given to professors for use on the first day of class. Unlike the "official" class roll which comes a few days later, this little list is not alphabetized. Now consider the first class meeting where the professor is meeting a new class and learning names. A student named Jane Smith raises her hand and asks if she is on the list. (She's not sure whether her registration has been processed.) "I'll check," responds the professor. "It is possible that some students are not on the list." What follows, of course, is that the professor now scans through the **entire list** to see whether the name "Jane Smith" appears. Since the list is not alphabetized, it is not until the complete list has been searched that the professor can be sure that Jane's name does not appear on it. If it does not, then the statement, "Some students are not on the list" is not just a possibility but actually true since at least one student is not on the list. The predicate term (which, of course, is not merely "on the list" but something more like "names which appear on the list") **is** distributed because something is said about every member of that class. Every name on the list is **not** the name of Jane Smith. The O proposition, then, does not distribute its subject term but definitely does distribute its predicate term. It says that every member of the predicate class is **not** one of the member(s) of S mentioned as "Some S."

To summarize the above discussion of distribution in convenient form, let us use the letter "d" for a class that is distributed and the letter "u" for a class that is undistributed. We can put the letter to the right and above the S or P rather in the way an exponent in math would be indicated. Thus, we can say that the following is a summary of what is and is not distributed in the four categorical propositions:

$$A = \text{All } S^d \text{ are } P^u$$
$$E = \text{No } S^d \text{ are } P^d$$
$$I = \text{Some } S^u \text{ are } P^u$$
$$O = \text{Some } S^u \text{ are not } P^d$$

Now that we have discussed the "standard form" of the four categorical propositions in some detail, it is worth noting that standard form has its limits. For one thing, not every statement in ordinary language uses a form of "to be" for its verb. This problem may be handled, as we have noted above, by changing the statement to include a predicate noun or noun phrase: ("run" to "are runners," etc.). Further, there are many other quantifiers in ordinary language besides "all," "no," and "some." "Every S is a P," for example, means the same as "All S are P." And of course, there are other particular quantifiers far more specific than "some": for example, "many," "most," "a few," "several," etc. The subtle but still significant differences here are beyond the ability of the individual categorical propositions to express. (Sometimes we can come closer by combining two categorical propositions; e.g. "Many people vote" could be expressed as **both** "Some people are voters" and "Some people are not voters.") The fact remains, though, that the four standard-form categorical propositions can be used to state an impressively large number of the kinds of things we say and reason about all the time; their usefulness can hardly be overstated.

Exercise:

I.   In a half-page to a page, discuss in your own words why it is correct, but inadequate, to say that Aristotle is the "father of logic."

II.   For each of the statements below, identify which kind of categorical proposition it is, what the subject and predicate classes are, and which classes are distributed. In most cases it will be necessary to change the statement slightly to be sure that nouns or noun phrases designate the classes and that the verb is a form of "to be."

1.   Some very small dogs bark loudly.

2.   All members of the history class are in the classroom.

3.   No students with scores under 60 passed the exam.

4.   Some people are not polite individuals who are respected by all.

5.   All political leaders in the United States interact regularly with the media.

6.   Some early hard drives for PC computers had only a 10 megabyte capacity.

7.   No pit bulls are animals which can be allowed to run freely in the neighborhood.

8.   Some basketball fans do not want a shot clock.

9.   Some influential political supporters of the president are business people.

10.   All severe weather warnings are broadcast on radio and television.

3.3 The Square of Opposition

All of our discussion so far has concerned the individual categorical propositions. We now know perhaps more than we wanted to know about each of them: its designating letter, its quality, its quantity, whether its subject and/or predicate terms are distributed. All of this is very interesting (?), but what can we **do** with this information? How do the categorical propositions help us with our reasoning? To begin to answer this question we need to consider how the four propositions relate to each other. What can we know about the truth or falsity of one of them if we know something about the truth or falsity of another one? The answer is that a good deal can be known, and this information is typically presented in a diagram known as the "Square of Opposition." In the square, the various "opposing" relationships of each categorical proposition to all of the others can be seen in a convenient way.

The following is the way the square is usually drawn:

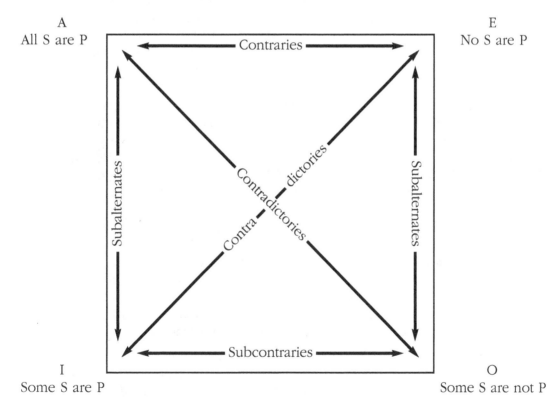

Figure 1

Notice that we have included diagonals in our square; this allows us to "move" directly from any one of the propositions to any other in a direct path. We can now use the square to discuss four crucial relationships:

(1) Contradictories. The pairs of categorical propositions which are at the diagonals of the square are known as the contradictories. There are thus two pairs of contradictories, A & O, and E & I. Contradictories are the direct opposite of each other, the "most opposed" of the various relationships on the square. Consider the A and O, "All S are P" and "Some S are not P." If one of them is true, the other is false, and vice-versa. Since "All dogs are animals" (A) is true, for example, we know that "Some dogs are not animals" (O) must necessarily be false. There is not even **one** dog that is not an animal. Similarly, if we know that "No dogs are cats" (E) is true, then its contradictory, "Some dogs are cats" (I) must be false. The contradictories cannot both be true with the same S and P, nor can they be false with the same S and P. Consider the belief that many people once had that all swans are white (this is a famous example!). When the first black swan was discovered in Australia, and it was confirmed that this really was a black swan and not just a white swan who had gotten stuck in a tar pit, then it was clear that the proposition "Some swans are not white things" (O) is true. This meant **logically** that the contradictory proposition "All swans are white things" (A) is false. We can use the same example for the other pair of contradictories: Since "Some swans are black things" (I) is now known to be true, its contradictory "No swans are black things" (E) must **logically** be false. Or let us begin with a false statement: "Some dogs are not animals." (O) Clearly its contradictory "All dogs are animals" (A) must be true.

Notice that we are no longer speaking about the individual categorical propositions but are engaging in logical arguments in which a conclusion is inferred from a single premiss. From "All S are P" we **conclude** that it is false that some S are not P. Such a "mini-argument" is sometimes called an "immediate inference," because we can move immediately from a single premiss to the conclusion. Let us return to the square to discover some other immediate inferences.

(2) Contraries. The two universal propositions (A and E) are known as the contraries. In one respect they are like the contradictories, in that they too cannot both be true with the same S and P. If it is true that all dogs are animals, then of course it must be false that no dogs are animals. But unlike the contradictories, the contraries can easily both be false with the same S and P. Consider the situation where the subject term is "dogs"

and the predicate term is "setters." The A proposition, "All dogs are setters" is false, but so is the E proposition, "No dogs are setters." On the other hand, the A proposition, "All dogs are cats" is false, yet the E proposition, "No dogs are cats" is true. Since the difference between these two examples is a difference in the content only, from the point of view of logic alone we **do not know** the truth value of the E when the A is false, or of the A when the E is false. To repeat, the contraries cannot both be true, but may or may not both be false, with the same S and P. Clearly, then, the contraries are quite different from the contradictories, which can neither be both true nor both false with the same S and P.

(3)   Subcontraries. The two particular propositions (I and O) are called the subcontraries. They are the opposite of the contraries in that they may be true together (that is, with the same S and P), but they cannot be false together. Consider first the situation in which one of the particular propositions is false: "Some dogs are cats." It is false, of course, to say that even one dog is a cat. We can immediately infer from the falsity of the I proposition that the O must be true: of course some dogs are not cats. (In fact, we would probably go on to make the stronger statement that no dogs are cats). For any S and P, we can immediately infer that if the I is false the O is true, and if the O is false the I is true. But consider now the case where one of the particular propositions is true. Take "Some dogs are setters." Its subcontrary, "Some dogs are not setters" is also true. But now take "Some dogs are animals." Its subcontrary, "Some dogs are not animals" is false. So from the point of view of logic alone we **do not know** the truth value of O when I is true, nor of the I when the O is true.

(4)   Subalternates. The two sides of the square—the A & I, and the E & O, are known as the subalternates. Sometimes the universal (A or E) of each pair is known as the "superaltern" and the particular (I or O) as the "subaltern." The relationship here can best be understood with a slogan: "Truth moves down, not up; falsity moves up, not down." What this means is simply that if a universal proposition is true, then that truth "moves (straight) down" the square to its subaltern. Specifically, if the A is true, then the I is true, and if the E is true, then the O is true. That this must be the case can be seen by looking at an example or two: Consider "All dogs are animals." This is a strong statement, saying that **every** dog is an animal. The subaltern, the I statement "Some dogs are animals," must be true because it is a "weaker" version of the same statement. It says that at least one dog is an animal, and if **all** dogs are animals then of course at least one of them

is an animal. Truth moves down, then, but it does not move up. Consider two true I propositions: "Some dogs are animals" and "Some dogs are setters." When we try to "move the truth up" to the superaltern, we find that "All dogs are animals" is true but "All dogs are setters" is false. In other words, given a true particular proposition, we **do not know** whether the corresponding universal proposition is true or false; it is unknown from the point of view of logic alone.

Looking at the other half of the slogan, "Falsity moves up, not down," consider the false particular statement, "Some dogs are cats." This says something very strong, namely, that not even one dog is a cat. Since "some dogs are cats" is false, then "All dogs are cats" must be false too. If not even **one** S is a P, then it would be ridiculous to suggest that **all** S's could be P's! So falsity moves (straight) "up" the square from subaltern to superaltern, but it does not move down. To see this, consider two false universal statements: "No dogs are animals" and "No dogs are setters." If we try to "move the falsity down" to the subalterns, we get "Some dogs are not animals" which is false, and "Some dogs are not setters," which is true. So from a false universal statement we cannot use logic alone to tell us whether its subalternate is true or false.

Note that what is said above applies to **both** pairs of subalternates, not just the cases selected to make the point. Specifically, "truth moves down, not up; falsity moves up, not down" means that:

Truth moves down:

> If the A is true, the I is true.
> If the E is true, the O is true.

Truth does not move up:

> If the I is true, the A is unknown.
> If the O is true, the E is unknown.

Falsity moves up:

> If the I is false, the A is false.
> If the O is false, the E is false.

Falsity does not move down:

> If the A is false, the I is unknown.
> If the E is false, the O is unknown.

If all this seems confusing (as well it might!), consider the following analogy. Think of the universal statements (A and E) as similar to requests to borrow a rather large amount of money, and think of the particular statements (I and O) as requests to borrow a small amount of money. Then think of truth as an approval of your request and falsity as a denial of your request. You can think of going to a bank, or perhaps simply of dealing with a friend. Now, let's go through the possibilities once again:

1. Truth moves down

   I ask my friend for $100 and he says he will give it to me. Then I say, "Wait a minute, it turns out I only need $5.00. Will you give me that instead?" The answer would of course be yes, because he has already agreed to loan me a larger amount. The approval (truth) of the stronger request moves "down" to the weaker or milder request.

2. Truth does not move up:

   I ask my friend for $5 and he says he will give it to me. Then I say, "Wait a minute, it turns out that I need $100. Will you give me that instead?" The answer is unknown; he might or might not be willing to give me the larger amount. The approval (truth) of a weaker request does not tell us one way or the other about a stronger request.

3. Falsity moves up:

   I ask my friend for $5 and he says no. Then I say, "Wait a minute, it turns out that I need $100. Will you give me that instead?" The answer would of course be no, because he had already turned down loaning me a smaller amount. The denial (falsity) of the weaker request moves "up" to the stronger request.

4. Falsity does not move down:

   I ask my friend for $100 and he says no. Then I say, "Wait a minute, it turns out that I only need $5. Will you give me that instead?" The answer is unknown; he might or might not be willing to give me the smaller amount. The denial (falsity) of a strong request does not tell us one way or the other about a weaker request.

Thus we have, in the four relationships of the Square of Opposition, several valid "immediate inferences" or one-premiss arguments. Are the ones just covered all there are? No, not quite. There are other immediate inferences which we will only sketch here; they are not "pure" like the ones above in that we have to do something to the quality, or the quantity, or the order of the subject and predicate terms, to get them to work. They are, however, worth mentioning:

(1) Conversion. This involves turning the subject and predicate classes around. It is valid only for the E and I propositions: From "No S are P" we can conclude that "No P are S." If the S class is completely excluded from the P class (No S are P), then it follows that no members of P could be S either. Further, from "Some S are P" we can conclude that "Some P are S." If at least one S is a P, then necessarily at least one P must be an S as well. Conversion does not work with the A and the O, except that we can convert the A and then **limit** the quantifier to the particular "some." Consider: From "All S are P" it certainly does not follow that "All P are S." (Think of "dogs" and "animals.") What **does** follow from "All S are P," though, is that **some** P are S. This sometimes called "conversion by limitation."

(2) Obversion. This is a two-part operation. First, we change the quality: affirmative to negative or negative to affirmative. Then we change the predicate class P to non-P, the class of everything that isn't P (sometimes called the "complementary class" of P). Thus, from "All dogs are animals" we can conclude that "No dogs are non-animals." Obversion does work for all four propositions:

"All S are P"	to	"No S are non-P"
"No S are P"	to	"All S are non-P"
"Some S are P"	to	"Some S are not non-P"
Some S are not P"	to	"Some S are non-P"

(3) Contraposition. This also involves two steps. First, we switch the positions of the subject and predicate terms as in conversion. Then we change each term to its complementary class: S to non-S and P to non-P. "All S are P" thus becomes "All non-P are non-S." It makes sense if you try an example: From "All dogs are animals" we can necessarily conclude that "All non-animals are non-dogs." Contraposition works only for the A and O propositions:

"All S are P"	to	"All non-P are non-S"
"Some S are not P"	to	"Some non-P are not non-S"

Contraposition does not work for the I proposition. It works for the E only if we limit the quantifier to the particular "some" as discussed under conversion above. Thus, from "No S are P" we can conclude that "**Some** non-P are not non-S." (Again, the proposition remains negative in quality, but the quantifier is particular rather than universal.)

Some interesting philosophical puzzles, beyond the scope of this book, arise from the various immediate inferences. Regarding contraposition, for example, a problem has arisen in the philosophy of science. We know that a statement like "All ravens are black" can be verified or confirmed each time someone observes a raven and notes that it is black. But the "contrapositive" of "All ravens are black," following the directions above, would be "All non-black things are non-ravens." This would seem to mean that anything which is non-black and also a non-raven (for example, a brown shoe or a white dog) would confirm "All ravens are black," since it confirms a statement which follows necessarily and immediately from "All ravens are black." Yet this seems ridiculous: if correct, then millions of ordinary everyday observations could confirm precise scientific hypotheses. The book you are holding in your hand confirms that all dogs are animals, for example, since it is a non-animal which is also a non-dog! This philosophical problem has been called the "paradox of confirmation," and you can find discussion of it (and the general issue of what it means to confirm or verify in science) in a philosophy of science textbook.

Exercise:

I.   Tell what can be immediately inferred from the information given in each case below. The answer will always be "true," "false," or "unknown."

1.   a.   If "All S are P" is **true,** then "No S are P" is:

b.   If "All S are P" is **false,** then "No S are P" is:

c.   If "All S are P" is **true,** then "Some S are P" is:

d.   If "All S are P" is **false,** then "Some S are P" is:

e.   If "All S are P" is **true,** then "Some S are not P" is:

f.   If "All S are P" if **false,** then "Some S are not P" is:

2.   a.   If "No S are P" is **true,** then "All S are P" is:

b.   If "No S are P" is **false,** then "All S are P" is:

c.   If "No S are P" is **true,** then "Some S are P" is:

d.   If "No S are P" is **false,** then "Some S are P" is:

e.   If "No S are P" is **true,** then "Some S are not P" is:

f.   If "No S are P" is **false,** then "Some S are not P" is:

3. a. If "Some S are P" is **true,** then "All S are P" is:

    b. If "Some S are P" is **false,** then "All S are P" is:

    c. If "Some S are P" is **true,** then "No S are P" is:

    d. If "Some S are P" is **false,** then "No S are P" is:

    e. If "Some S are P" is **true,** then "Some S are not P" is:

    f. If "Some S are P" is **false,** then "Some S are not P" is:

4. a. If "Some S are not P" is **true,** then "All S are P" is:

    b. If "Some S are not P" is **false,** then "All S are P" is:

    c. If "Some S are not P" is **true,** then "No S are P" is:

    d. If "Some S are not P" is **false,** then "No S are P" is:

    e. If "Some S are not P" is **true,** then "Some S are P" is:

    f. If "Some S are not P" is **false,** then "Some S are P" is:

II.   Note that in the above exercise, the letters S and P are used throughout to designate the subject and predicate classes. The answers would be the same regardless of the content, that is, regardless of what classes S and P actually stood for. In a paragraph or two, explain why this is the case.

3.4 A Sketch of Some Related Philosophical Issues

Logic is a branch of philosophy, and as such its issues are philosophical ones. Philosophy questions basic assumptions about reality, about knowledge, about values. To deal with almost any topic at one level means making assumptions which at a deeper level, can be called into question. In this section we will offer a sketch of a philosophical issue which relates directly to categorical logic as presented above.

This issue centers around the nature and use of language, a major philosophical concern in the twentieth century. When we use terms such as "dogs," "brown dogs," "dogs that run in my yard," etc., it is reasonably clear that these terms in some way refer or point to classes or groups of things which we can recognize. Such things exist, and at least **one** function of language is to describe classes of things that exist. One important issue, brought to the forefront of philosophical discussion by Ludwig Wittgenstein in the middle part of the twentieth century, is the question of what other functions language has in addition to "naming" classes of things. Wittgenstein notes that there are many and various uses of language—directing, questioning, expressing feelings, and so on (his work has influenced the discussion on language in Chapter One of this book, for example), and warns that it is too narrow a perspective to think of **all** language as having a "naming" function, as it does when we say that the word "dogs" names a class.

Even if we confine ourselves to language which **does** have the function of naming things, it is still unclear what is going on when there are **no members of the class named.** What exactly are we talking about when we use the words "ghosts," "unicorns," "mermaids," etc.? Since there probably are no members of those classes, it would seem that **any** proposition about such things is false. Some philosophers have said that a proposition cannot be true unless what it talks about really exists. If we take this position, then any proposition about unicorns is false since there are no unicorns. On the other hand, since stories about unicorns, ghosts, etc., contain rather precise descriptions of what such things would be like **if** they existed, it would seem that some statements about these "things" are true. "Unicorns have one horn" would seem to be true, for example, while "unicorns have two horns" would seem to be false.

What does this general problem have to do with categorical propositions? Well, consider the square of opposition again. Let's say that the subject class S is "unicorns" and the predicate class P is "one-horned animals." If we take the position that a proposition cannot be true unless what it talks about exists, then in this case **all four** of the categorical propositions would be false: "All unicorns are one-horned animals," "No unicorns are one-horned animals," "Some unicorns are one-horned animals," and "Some unicorns are not one-horned animals." What has become of the contradictories and the other relationships of the square of opposition? It would seem that these relationships depend upon assuming the existence of members of the classes they discuss. One proposal often adopted by logicians is to say that the particular propositions (I and O) must, in order to be true, refer to what exists. "Some unicorns are one-horned animals" would not then be true, since it says that **at least one** unicorn is a one-horned animal and there are no unicorns to make that true. But this proposal goes on to hold that the universal propositions (A and E) need not require the existence of members of their classes in order to be true. In such a case, we could say that "All unicorns are one-horned animals" is true since this is the way unicorns are described in mythology and folklore. Even if we make this assumption, we are still treading on thin ice when we ask just what it is that makes a universal proposition true when it refers to such "things" as unicorns. Is it true because of the **stories** about unicorns? Because of a hypothetical situation, e.g. **if** there were any unicorns, **then** all of them would have one horn? Or because of a shared context in which the listener assumes a mythological realm in judging the truth of such statements? This problem is sometimes called the "problem of existential import," and while we will not discuss it further, it is worth noting this rather thorny philosophical issue lurking beneath the surface of our neat, orderly and useful square of opposition.

3.5 Symbolizing and Diagramming the Categorical Propositions

The categorical propositions can be symbolized and diagrammed. There are several ways this can be done—especially the diagramming—but we will look in this section at the way logicians usually do it. This, naturally, will be a way which is useful for examining the logical relations among the propositions.

The way we symbolize the categorical propositions depends upon the notion of an empty class, or a class which has no members. This concept was discussed by George Boole, a nineteenth-century mathematician whose work has had a major role in the discussion of the problem of existential import. If we take class S and we wish to make the statement that there are no members of this class, a symbolic way to say this would be S = 0. This says, in other words, that there are no members of S, that the class of S is empty, or "equal to nothing." To make a **true** statement, let us take the class of unicorns and represent it with a capital U. We could then say U = 0, and this would be a true statement: There are no unicorns. What if, on the other hand, we wanted to say that there **are** members of a class? Take the class of dogs, for instance. To say that there are some dogs is to say that the class of dogs **is not empty,** so we use the inequality sign ($\neq$) and we say D $\neq$ 0. We are saying, in other words, that the class of dogs does **not** have no members. However awkward this may sound in English, this amounts to saying that the class of dogs does have at least one member.

Now, consider the E proposition: No S are P. This says that nothing is both S and P; nothing which is S is also P. This can be symbolized by saying **SP = 0:** The class of SP (that which is both S and P) has no members. There are no SP's. Taking the true statement, "No dogs are cats," and symbolizing the classes by D and C respectively, we can symbolically say **DC = 0.** There are no dog-cats.

The I proposition, Some S are P, is of course the contradictory of the E. It is thus symbolized in a way that brings out this fact. The I says that the class of SP (that which is both S and P), **does** have at least one member. The class is not empty, so we say symbolically **SP $\neq$ 0.** Taking a true statement such as "Some dogs are setters," and using the letters D and S, we can say **DS $\neq$ 0.** Thus the E and I propositions are symbolized such that exactly what one says, the other denies: **SP = 0** (E), and **SP $\neq$ 0** (I). This is, of course, what we expect of the contradictories.

To examine the A and O propositions we need to return to the concept of the complement of a class. The **complement** of a class is the class of everything which is not a member of the original class. The complement of the class of dogs is non-dogs. Everything in the world which is not a dog belongs to the class of non-dogs. Our convention for symbolizing the **complement** of a class is to put a bar over the letter for that class, so non-S would be written $\overline{S}$ and non-P would be written $\overline{P}$. Now consider the A proposition, "All S are P." It says that every S is a P, and this of course means that there are no S's which are not P's. In other words, the class of everything which is S and not P is **empty,** has no members. We can thus symbolize the A proposition

S$\overline{\text{P}}$ = 0; the class of what is both S and non-P is empty. For a true A proposition, take "All dogs are animals," and use the letters D and A for the classes: **D$\overline{\text{A}}$ = 0.**

The O proposition, "Some S are not P," is of course the contradictory of the A, and our symbolic notation should make this point. We say saying in the O that the class of everything which is S and not P is **not empty;** that is, it has at least one member. We thus say **S$\overline{\text{P}}$ ≠ 0.**

To sum up the symbolic notations for our four categorical propositions:

A:	**S$\overline{\text{P}}$ = 0**	E:	**SP = 0**
I:	**SP ≠ 0**	O:	**S$\overline{\text{P}}$ ≠ 0**

One might wonder what purpose is served by symbolizing the categorical propositions. In fact, what we are about to do—create "Venn Diagrams" of each proposition—is far more important than the symbolic notations just discussed and in addition can be learned independently of these notations. There is a considerable advantage, however, to doing both, as each helps to make the other clearer. You can judge for yourself whether this is true after reading about the diagrams.

Venn Diagrams are named after the nineteenth-century mathematician John Venn. Though there are many variations on them and many uses for them outside of categorical logic, we will naturally concentrate on their use for our purposes. We have been talking all through this chapter about two classes, the subject class S and the predicate class P. Each of the four categorical propositions says something about to what extent the two classes "overlap," that is, to what extent S is or is not included in P. In drawing a Venn diagram for a categorical proposition, we represent each class with a circle. We overlap the circles slightly so that an area is available for every possible combination:

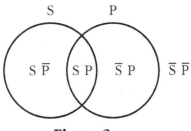

Figure 2

Notice that we have labelled the diagram using the notation we just discussed. The label **$\overline{\text{S}}\overline{\text{P}}$** represents everything in the universe outside the two diagrams, everything which is non-S and also non-P. (Recall that the bar above the letter refers to the complement or everything which is **not** a member of the class.) On the other hand, the label **SP** in the middle of the diagram labels the area which is common to both circles, everything which is both S and P. The left-hand part of the S circle is labelled **SP̄,** because this section is S but is non-P. The right-hand part of the P circle is labelled **S̄P** because this section is non-S but is P. In other words, we have here a basic schema for a Venn diagram of any of the categorical propositions. We are thus ready to turn this schema into the actual diagrams for each of the four propositions.

Let us begin with the E proposition, No S are P. As we know all too well by now, this says that every member of the S class is excluded from the P class. The convention we use to show **exclusion** in a Venn Diagram is shading. Shading an area eliminates the possibility of there being anything in that area. Thus we shade the middle part of our diagram, the part which is common to S and P:

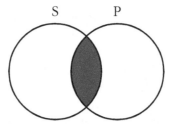

Figure 3

The diagram says that there are no common members of both the S and P classes. What is shaded is **gone;** there can be nothing there. So the only part of the S class which can possibly have any members is the left-hand part of the S circle, the part completely outside the P circle. No S are P. Note, also that our symbolic notation for the E proposition was **SP = 0.** The diagram confirms this, because we took the SP section of the diagram and made it "0"; that is, we shaded it to show that nothing can be in it. Thus the diagram shows visually what our symbolic notation says.

Consider now the contradictory of the E proposition, namely the I proposition: Some S are P. Since the contradictories exactly deny one another, we would expect this to exhibit itself in some way in the diagram. This is precisely what happens. The middle part of the diagram, the part common to both S and P which we shaded in diagramming the E proposition, now has an "X" in it when we diagram the I proposition:

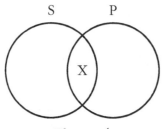

Figure 4

In a Venn diagram the "X" works in the same way it does in, say, a pirate's treasure map. It says that **something is there,** that there exists at least one member in the part of the diagram where it appears. This, of course, is the same way we use the English word "some." Notice, now, that the E and I diagrams are, as we had expected, exactly the opposite of one another. The same area which is shaded or eliminated in the E diagram has something in it in the I diagram. Thus the E and I will always have opposite truth values; if one is true the other must be false and vice-versa. Notice also that our symbolic notation for the I proposition corresponds nicely to the diagram: **SP ≠ 0** says that the "SP" area (the area common to S and P) is not empty or not "equal to zero." The X in this area confirms this by saying that something is indeed there.

Now let's look at the other pair of contradictories, starting with the "A" proposition: All S are P. This says, of course, that all members of S are members of P. Thus there are no members of S which are not members of P, so we shade the left-hand part of the diagram to show this. In other words, we use shading to eliminate the portion of the S circle which is outside the P circle to say that there is nothing there. Any members of S would have to be in the portion of the S circle which remains, and this portion is entirely inside the P circle: All S are P. Once again we can see that our symbolic notation and our Venn diagram correspond well. Our notation for the A proposition was **S$\overline{P}$ = 0.** This says there are no members of the **S$\overline{P}$** class, and the diagram says the same thing by using shading to eliminate the possibility of there being any members of that class.

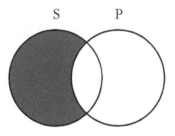

Figure 5

Looking finally at the O proposition, Some S are not P, we note again that it says that there exists at least one member of S outside the P class. Our diagram reflects this by placing an X in the left-hand portion of the S circle outside the P circle:

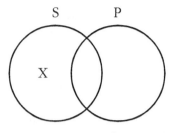

Figure 6

This says that there exists something which is S but is not P. This corresponds to our symbolic notation for the O which was **S$\overline{P}$ ≠ 0,** because it says that the class of what is S and not P is **not empty.** In other words, there **is something** in the **S$\overline{P}$** class. Note that the A and O diagrams are indeed the opposite of each other since the two propositions are contradictories. The **S$\overline{P}$** section which we shaded in the A (since it can have nothing in it) contains an X is the O (since it does have something in it).

Thus the four categorical propositions can be symbolized, diagrammed, and otherwise dissected as we have seen in detail. We are now ready to see how the knowledge we have obtained thus far can be put to use in analyzing and judging the success of that model of classical logic, the categorical syllogism.

Exercise:

1.   Describe in a brief paragraph what SP = 0 says and how the diagram for the E proposition shows this in a pictorial way.

2.   Describe in a brief paragraph how the Venn diagrams help to bring out the meaning of the relationships we call "contradictories."

3.   Draw some Venn diagrams for simple propositions such as "No dogs are cats," "Some birds are runners," "All logic students study syllogisms," and "Some collies do not bark." Do the necessary translations to get your propositions into standard form, then pick appropriate capital letters to represent your subject and predicate classes. For even more fun, write the appropriate symbolic notation for each of your propositions. You may use the ones suggested and/or make up your own.

3.6 Putting the Pieces Together: Categorical Syllogisms

Everything that has been said so far has been about categorical propositions. We have talked about various ways to represent them, the relationships between and among them, and what can be inferred about their truth value when certain assumptions are made. All of this, though important, was done to pave the way for our consideration of the categorical syllogism. "Syllogism," a word which comes to us directly from the Greek, was defined by Aristotle as "discourse in which, certain things being stated, something other than what is stated follows of necessity from their being so."[1]

In more modern language we can say that a syllogism is any deductive argument with two premisses and a conclusion. What particularly interests us, however, are not syllogisms in general but **categorical** syllogisms. We can define a categorical syllogism as a deductive argument which meets all of the following requirements:

1. Consists of two premisses and a conclusion
2. All of its statements are standard-form categorical propositions
3. Mentions a total of three classes
4. Each class is mentioned twice, and in two different propositions

Let us consider a typical categorical syllogism:

> All dogs are animals.
> No rocks are animals.
> ∴ No rocks are dogs.

All of the four requirements are met: (1) There are two premisses and a conclusion. (2) All three statements are standard form categorical propositions. The two premisses are "A" and "E" propositions, and the conclusion is another "E" proposition. (3) A total of three classes are mentioned: dogs, animals, and rocks. (4) Each of these classes is mentioned twice. "Dogs" appears in the first premiss and the conclusion, "animals" in the two premisses, and "rocks" in the second premiss and the conclusion. So the above argument is clearly a categorical syllogism.

Like individual categorical propositions, categorical syllogisms also have a standard form. The above example is already arranged in standard form and is ready for testing via the methods we will soon be learning. But note that in ordinary speaking and writing, we frequently use categorical syllogisms but do not necessarily arrange them in standard form. We use words which indicate which of our statements are premisses or conclusions, and we arrange our arguments in several different ways. (See Chapter One for a fuller discussion of this point.) Thus for the categorical syllogism above, any of the following would be perfectly acceptable in ordinary conversation:

---

[1] Aristotle, *Prior Analytics,* Book I, Chapter I.

No rocks are dogs, since all dogs are animals and no rocks are
   animals.
No rocks are animals, so no rocks are dogs since all dogs are
   animals.
Because no rocks are animals and all dogs are animals, no rocks
   are dogs.

This argument happens to be valid, and it is valid regardless of how we state it, so long as we make clear which statements are the premisses and which the conclusion. To **demonstrate** its validity, however, we need to put the argument in standard form. The first step in doing this is to identify the conclusion, and this clearly is "No rocks are dogs." The subject term of the conclusion is "rocks" and the predicate term is "dogs." **By definition, we refer to the subject and predicate terms of the conclusion of a categorical syllogism as the "minor" and "major" terms of the syllogism, respectively.** So "rocks" is the minor term and "dogs" is the major term of the syllogism. In standard form we must state the premisses first and then the conclusion, but which premiss shall we state first? The answer is straightforward: **the premiss stated first is the premiss which contains the major term.** Thus "All dogs are animals" is stated first, since it contains the major term, "dogs." We call this premiss the "major premiss" of the syllogism **because** it contains the major term. The other premiss, of course, contains the minor term, "rocks." This premiss is stated second and is called the minor premiss. So standard form calls for the following order of premisses and conclusion:

Major Premiss (contains the major term)
Minor Premiss (contains the minor term)
Conclusion (contains, in order, the minor and major terms)

You may have noticed that there is one term which we have not yet discussed. This is "animals," and it appears in both premisses but not in the conclusion. The term that appears in both premisses is called the **middle term** of the syllogism. We often list the three terms of the syllogism using the letters S, P, M, for the minor, major, and middle terms respectively. (S and P are used because the minor term is the **s**ubject and the major term is the **p**redicate of the conclusion.) Now we can complete our listing of the positions of our terms in standard form:

Major Premiss (contains major and middle terms—P and M)
Minor Premiss (contains minor and middle terms—S and M)
Conclusion (contains, in order, minor and major terms—S and P)

Notice that the schema we have just stated fits the categorical syllogism we are discussing:

All dogs are animals.
No rocks are animals.
∴ No rocks are dogs.

This syllogism's major premiss is a universal affirmative or A proposition. Its minor premiss is a universal negative or E proposition, and its conclusion is also an E proposition. We refer to the **mood** of a categorical syllogism by naming the letters of the propositions which form, in order, the major premiss, minor premiss, and conclusion of the syllogism. So the above syllogism's mood is AEE.

To give the mood of a syllogism is to give a good deal of information. Just by hearing that the mood is AEE we already know that the syllogism under consideration will have a major premiss, "All . . . are . . . ," a minor premiss "No . . . are . . . ," and a conclusion "No . . . are . . ." But notice that nothing in the above discussion tells us that the middle term must appear in the predicate position of the major and minor premiss as it does in the categorical syllogism we are considering at the moment. We have noted carefully that in the conclusion, the minor and major terms must appear **in order,** with the minor term in the subject place and the major term in the predicate place. There is no similar requirement for the order of the terms which appear in the two premisses. To spell it out, the terms in the major premiss can be arranged in either of these ways:

Major term P—Middle term M

or

Middle term M—Major term P

Similarly in the minor premiss, the terms can be arranged in either of these ways:

Minor term S—Middle term M

or

Middle term M—Minor term S

Now a categorical syllogism contains two premisses, and since each of these two premisses can have its terms arranged in either of these ways, there are a total of four combinations (or "figures," as they are called) in a categorical syllogism:

First Figure:

Major Premiss: Middle Term M—Major Term P
Minor Premiss: Minor Term S—Middle Term M
Conclusion: Minor Term S—Major Term P

Second Figure:

> Major Premiss: Major Term P—Middle Term M
> Minor Premiss: Minor Term S—Middle Term M
> Conclusion: Minor Term S—Major Term P

Third Figure:

> Major Premiss: Middle Term M—Major Term P
> Minor Premiss: Middle Term M—Minor Term S
> Conclusion: Minor Term S—Major Term P

Fourth Figure:

> Major Premiss: Major Term P—Middle Term M
> Minor Premiss: Middle Term M—Minor Term S
> Conclusion: Minor Term S—Major Term P

A little reflection will show that these are the only possible combinations given the requirements. The conclusion, as you can see above, is the same in every case; the order of the terms never varies. The major premiss always contains the major term and the minor premiss always contains the minor term. There is always a middle term which appears in both premisses. The only variable is in the order in which the terms appear in the premisses. We can state the four figures in a more concise way by using simply the letters S, P, M:

First Figure:	Second Figure:	Third Figure:	Fourth Figure
M–P	P–M	M–P	P–M
S–M	S–M	M–S	M–S
∴ S–P	∴ S–P	∴ S–P	∴ S–P

These figures can be easily remembered by noting visually the arrangement of the M's. You might try using a highlighter to mark through the M's and you will notice the "shape" that emerges. Some see a bow-tie, a shirt-collar, or a person with out-stretched arms—use your imagination, form a mental image, and you'll never forget the figures!

There is a good reason we take time to discuss moods and figures. The two together provide a "code" which allows us to look at the form of **any categorical syllogism** at all. Think of the codes we use on computers to bring up certain sets of data. The moods and figures are like that. Let us go back once again to the syllogism we were discussing:

> All dogs are animals.
> No rocks are animals.
> ∴ No rocks are dogs.

We said above that the mood of this syllogism is AEE, because the major premiss, minor premiss, and conclusion are A, E, and E propositions in that order. We can now go on to say that this syllogism is in the Second Figure, because its middle term ("animals") appears in the predicate of both the major and minor premisses. Thus the combination of Mood AEE in the Second Figure (normally written AEE-2), gives us the unique form or logical structure of this categorical syllogism:

> All P are M.
> No S are M.
> ∴ No S are P.

AEE-2 is valid, and in the next section we will see how its validity can be proved. But notice now what this means. We noted in Chapter One that the validity of a deductive argument is a function of its form and not its content. Since AEE-2 is a valid form, this means that any argument in this form is valid. To say it another way, any content at all when presented in the form of AEE-2 will produce a valid argument. Any terms we substitute for letters S, P, and M will give us an argument such that **if** the premisses are both true **then** the conclusion will be true (this is what a valid argument is). In the argument above we really have true premisses and a true conclusion and thus our argument is not only valid but sound (recall from Chapter One that a sound argument is a valid argument in which all the premisses really are true). One might, of course, produce an argument in form AEE-2 in which one or both of the premisses and/or the conclusion are false. But to say that AEE-2 is valid is to guarantee that when we use this form, **if** our premisses are both true **then** our conclusion must be true.

Every standard-form categorical syllogism has a mood and figure. How many mood/figure combinations are there? Consider: There are four categorical propositions (A,E,I,O). Any one of these four could be the major premiss of a syllogism, any one could be the minor premiss, and any one could be the conclusion. So there are 4 × 4 × 4 or 64 different **moods.** (A complete listing would look like this: AAA, AAE, AAI, AAO, AEA, AEE, . . . all the way to OOO.) However, each of these 64 moods could appear with any of the four **figures,** so there are 64 × 4 or 256 different categorical syllogisms. Each of these 256 syllogisms is either valid or invalid (far more are invalid than valid). This makes our next task both clear and somewhat urgent: How can we prove the validity or invalidity of a given categorical syllogism?

Exercise:

I.   In a brief essay, explain how moods and figures are important to the logician in reference to the validity or invalidity of categorical syllogisms.

II.   Each of the following is a categorical syllogism stated in ordinary language. Translate each to standard form. (Keep in mind that the first step is to be sure which statement is the conclusion.) Once you have the syllogism in standard form, name its mood and figure. (NOTE: Some of these syllogisms are valid and some are not. Don't worry about this **yet.**)

1. Some students learn logic easily, because some students are capable of hard work and all those capable of hard work learn logic easily.

2. Some people who reason analytically are mathematicians, and because all logic students reason analytically, some logic students are mathematicians.

3. All collies are dogs, so some animals are collies, since all dogs are animals.

4. No computers have minds, for all people have minds and no computers are people.

5. Some children are not stupid, so, because all stupid people make mistakes, some children do not make mistakes.

6. No TV stars are "just plain folks," so some "just plain folks" are virtuous people, since some TV stars are virtuous people.

7. Some dogs are not cats, since some dogs are intelligent and no cats are intelligent.

3.7 Testing Categorical Syllogisms for Validity: Venn Diagrams

Recall from section 3.5 that the Venn Diagram for each categorical proposition is a picture of what that proposition says. Each of the four Venn Diagrams for the individual propositions contains two overlapping circles, one for each class. Shading, the letter x, and blank space are all used to illustrate what each proposition says: shading eliminates an area so that nothing could be in it, the letter x says that something exists in the area where the x appears, and blank space indicates simply that this space is available and might or might not have something in it.

Each categorical **syllogism,** of course, works with a total of three classes. A Venn Diagram of a categorical syllogism would thus need to have three circles, all of them overlapping:

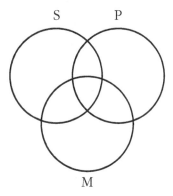

Figure 7

Notice that the circles are labelled S, P, and M, for the minor term, major term, and middle term respectively. All Venn Diagrams of syllogisms begin with this basic schema. (Some logicians prefer to place the M circle above rather than below the S and P circles, but all three must still overlap.)

To understand where we go from here, let's briefly review what a valid argument is. It is an argument with a form such that **if** the premisses are all true, **then** necessarily the conclusion must be true. The premisses "force" the conclusion, we might say. The conclusion is "automatic" given the premisses. Now a Venn diagram of a categorical syllogism is simply a picture of the two premisses. We make the appropriate marks (shading, an X, or leaving an area blank) until the circles "say" what the premisses "say." Then we stop and look. Do the circles also say what the conclusion says? If so, the argument is valid. If not, it isn't.

Let's put it another way and then get to work with some examples. A valid argument has a form such that if all its premisses are true then its conclusion is true. A Venn Diagram of any argument is a picture of that argument's premisses being true. If the argument is **valid,** then that picture is also a picture of the conclusion being true. We draw the premisses onto our circles, and then we look to see whether what we have drawn is also what the conclusion says. Either it is or it isn't. The argument is thus either valid or invalid.

We begin with AAA-1, sometimes cited as the premiere example of a valid categorical syllogism. Following our discussion of mood and figure above, we know that AAA-1 will be the following syllogism:

All M are P.
All S are M.
∴ All S are P.

We now make our circles "say" what each premiss says. Beginning with the major premiss, we direct our attention to the M and P circles, ignoring the S circle for the moment. The major premiss says that all M are P, which is to say that **there is no M which is not P.** We thus shade (to eliminate) the part of the M circle which is outside P:

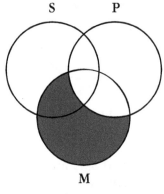

Figure 8

This diagram now "says" that everything which is in the M class is also in the P class. It says this because everything in the M class which was outside the P class is shaded out; there **could** not be anything there. All M are P.

Now we look at the minor premiss: All S are M. Ignoring the P circle and looking only at the S and M circles, we see that in order to show what the minor premiss says, we must shade or eliminate whatever part of the S circle lies outside the M circle. This we do as follows:

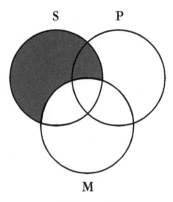

Figure 9

This now says that everything which is S is M, since there is no S left unshaded outside of M. Putting the two diagrams together we get the following:

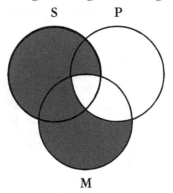

Figure 10

Normally this complete diagram is the only one we draw; we simply put the diagrams of the major and minor premisses together on the same set of circles. For purposes of clarity, we diagrammed the premisses separately in this first example. What we have now is a complete diagram of AAA-1. We have, in other words, a picture of what the premisses say, and this is all we ever diagram. How do we interpret the diagram to decide whether the argument is valid? We simply look to see whether our picture of what the premisses say is also a picture of what the conclusion says. Either it is or it isn't. Well, the conclusion says "All S are P," so our question is whether this diagram shows all of the remaining part of the S circle to be in the P circle. Remembering that the shaded parts have been eliminated altogether, we can see that **the entire available (non-shaded) part** of the S circle is indeed inside the P circle. Thus what the conclusion says is shown here, and yet we did not draw the conclusion; we drew only the premisses. The argument is shown to be valid because **our picture of the premisses automatically produced a picture of the conclusion.**

Now let's look at a different argument:

> All P are M.
> All S are M.
> ∴ All S are P.

We can see that this form is AAA-2. (Both premisses and the conclusion are A propositions, and the middle term is in the predicate of both premisses.)

Looking first at the P and M circles, we shade out the portion of the P circle which lies outside the M circle. All of the P circle that remains is now inside the M circle, and the diagram now shows the major premiss of the argument (All P are M). To show the minor premiss, we look at both the S and M circles, and we shade out the portion of the S circle which lies outside the M circle. What is left of the S circle is now entirely inside the M circle, just as the minor premiss says (All S are M). The two pieces of shading we did combine to produce the following diagram:

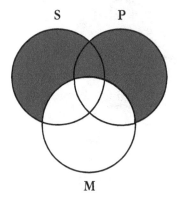

Figure 11

This diagram is a picture of the premisses of AAA-2. If AAA-2 is valid, this picture of the premisses will also be a picture of the conclusion; if invalid, it will not be. The conclusion of AAA-2 says "All S are P." This would mean that whatever portion of the S circle remains unshaded will **all** be part of the P circle. Is this what we see? Well, we do notice that the middle part of the entire diagram (sometimes called the "shield") does remain unshaded and is part of both S and P. But significantly, we also notice that the left-middle part of the diagram is unshaded, and this area is part of S but **not** part of P. The fact that this section is unshaded means that it is not eliminated; something **could** be there. Thus it is not true that all S are P, because there is some "available" S which is outside the P circle. So what the conclusion says is not what we see, and thus the diagram shows that AAA-2 is invalid.

Look back at the two diagrams we have done so far. AAA-1 is valid because its conclusion is what we see: all the available S (that is, the part of S that is unshaded) is in the P circle, so all S are P. AAA-2 is invalid because we do not see what its conclusion says. There is available S outside the P circle, even though the conclusion says that all S are P. Keep in mind, also, that what we have just shown is that **any** categorical syllogism of form AAA-1 is valid and **any** categorical syllogism of form AAA-2 is invalid. Thus the significance of what we are doing goes far beyond the few circles and pieces of shading we have drawn.

Now consider another mood and figure, EIO-4:

No P are M.
Some M are S.
∴ Some S are not P.

This time, before we begin our diagram, we notice that we will be doing a piece of shading (for the major premiss which is universal) and we will also be drawing an X (for the minor premiss which is particular). We recall that the way to diagram a particular proposition (which says "some") is to draw an X. It is a rule in drawing Venn diagrams that **when the premisses include both a universal and a particular proposition, always diagram the universal proposition first.** In other words, do the necessary shading before drawing the X. The reason for this is that the shading shows us what areas are ruled out, what areas could not possibly have anything in them. Should we draw the X first, we might put it in an area which we find out later is ruled out. (Farmers fence their fields before releasing the animals into the fields.) In the case of EIO-4, of course, we will be diagramming the major premiss first as we have done before, but this is because it is the universal premiss, not because it is the major. If our syllogism were IEO-4, we would still diagram the universal premiss first, but in this case it would be the minor.

We begin, then, by shading the common area shared by P and M. This area is the "football" shape which those two circles share. When this is done our diagram says that no P are M. Next, to diagram "Some M are S," we look at the common area shared by M and S. Notice that part of this common area (the middle part or "shield" of the entire diagram) has been eliminated by our shading. The only place left for the X we must draw is in the middle-left section of our diagram. Thus our final picture of this syllogism looks like this:

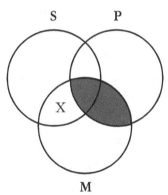

Figure 12

Does this diagram of the **premisses** of EIO-4 also show the **conclusion?** If so, the argument is valid; otherwise it is not. Well, the conclusion says "Some S are not P." For this conclusion to be shown in the diagram, an X would have to appear in some part of the S circle which at the same time is not part of the P circle. We can see that the X which does appear in the diagram fulfills this requirement: it is in the middle-left part of the diagram, and it is in the S circle while being outside the P circle. Thus what the conclusion says should be there **is** there, and again (as in AAA-

1) we produced this conclusion not by setting out to draw it, but by limiting our-selves to drawing the premisses. So a picture of the premisses is a picture of the conclusion, and the argument is valid.

Our next example is the following:

> Some P are not M.
> All M are S.
> ∴ Some S are not P.

We can see that the mood here is OAO, and with the middle term M arranged as it is (predicate of the major premiss, subject of the minor premiss), we have the fourth figure. Recall our rule in the previous example: where our two premisses are a uni-versal and a particular, we must always diagram the universal premiss first (i.e. we must do the shading before drawing the X). Thus we will begin this time with the **minor** premiss, "All M are S," since it is the universal one. Looking at the M and S circles, we shade the part of the M circle which lies outside the S circle. This leaves only a small football-shaped part of the M circle still "available," and this part lies entirely inside the S circle. Now we look at the major premiss, "Some P are not M." We know that we must put an X somewhere in the part of the P circle which is out-side the M circle. But notice that this part of the P circle partly overlaps with the S circle. In other words, part of the P-outside-M is S and part isn't S. Since we are to draw just one X, where should we put it? If we put it **inside** S, then we are saying that this P which is not M is **also S,** and this assumes more than we were told. If we put it **outside** S, then we are saying that this P which is not M is **also not S,** again assum-ing more than we were told. In a case like this, where a line from another circle is found within our area for the X, we simply **put the X on the line.** This way we are clearly showing what the major premiss says ("Some P are not M"), but we are not taking a stand one way or the other on what the major premiss does not tell us (whether this P which is not M is also S or not). Our diagram, then, will look like this:

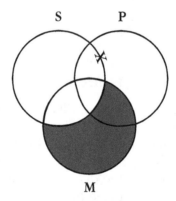

Figure 13

Now, what about the validity of OAO-4? The conclusion says "Some S are not P." For this conclusion to be shown on the diagram, we would have to find an X which is definitely in the S circle and at the same time definitely not in the P circle. Is this what we see? Well, we certainly see an X. Is it in the S circle? Maybe, and maybe not. It is on the line of the S circle, which says that it might be inside the S circle but it might not. The X, remember, stands for just **one** thing (the minimal meaning of "some"). The fact that the X is on the line doesn't mean that a little of it is both inside and outside the S circle. It means rather that **this one thing** might be either inside or outside the S circle. If it should "really" be outside the S circle (in the area just to the right of the line where we put it), then "Some S are not P" could not possibly be true since there would be no X anywhere in the S circle. (Remember, a particular statement is not shown to be true in a diagram unless there is an X to represent "some"; blank space alone merely means there **could** be something there.) Of course, if the X should "really" be inside the S circle (in the area just to the left of where we put it), then "Some S are not P" would still be false because this same X is still in the P circle. For "Some S are not P" to be shown on the diagram, an X would have to appear somewhere in the left part of the S circle, the part outside the P circle. And in **neither** case would our X show that. Since the area of S which is outside P is blank, it is always possible that something could be there, but there is no reason one way or the other to think that something actually is there. So the premisses of this argument do not make the conclusion necessary. A picture of the premisses produces a picture in which the conclusion might or might not be true, and this, unfortunately, is not enough to meet the strict requirement for validity ("if the premisses are true, the conclusion is **necessarily** true").

Consider one more example: OOO-2. Since all of the propositions are particular negatives or O's, we know that we will be drawing two X's for our premisses. We also know that we will be looking for an X when we check the conclusion. Let us first state the syllogism:

> Some P are not M.
> Some S are not M.
> ∴ Some S are not P.

Since both premisses are particular propositions requiring an X, it makes no difference which we draw first. (The only time this makes a difference is in the case where one premiss is universal and the other particular.) Let us begin with the major premiss, "Some P are not M." This tells us to put an X somewhere in the P circle such that it is also **not** in the M circle. This would be the "upper" part of the P circle, and we see that there is a line (the S circle) going through the area where we are told to draw the X. Since we have no idea whether the "some" P which is not M **is or is not S,** we put our X on this line. We have thus shown that some P is definitely not M, and that this P may or may not be S. Thus our major premiss is shown on the diagram.

To move on to the minor premiss, "Some S are not M," we know that we will be drawing an X in the portion of the S circle which is **not** in the M circle. This would be the "upper" part of the S circle, and we see once again that there is a line (the P circle) going through the area where we are told to draw the X. Since we do not know whether the "some" S which is not M **is or is not P,** we put our X on this line. Thus we have said that some S is definitely not M, and that this S may or may not be P. Both premisses are now shown on the diagram.

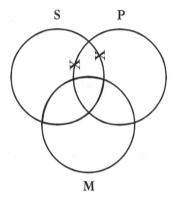

S   P

M

Figure 14

Is OOO-2 valid? Our diagram shows both premisses; does it show the conclusion, "Some S are not P"? If it does, then there would be an X somewhere in the S circle which is also definitely not in the P circle. Does either of our X's qualify? Well, the X we drew for the major premiss (the one on the right as you look at both X's) certainly does not qualify. The reason is that **whichever side** of the line it is "really" on is still within the P circle, and our conclusion asks us to look for an X which is **not** P. What about the other X, the one on the left? Well, it certainly qualifies as "some S": whichever side of the line it is "really" on, it is in the S circle. But is it "not P" as our conclusion requires? Unfortunately we can't know for sure. Depending upon which side of the line it is "really" on, it **might** not be P, but on the other hand it **might** be P. But our conclusion does not say that some S **might** not be P; it says that definitely, necessarily, some S **is not P.** The diagram does not show the necessity of the conclusion, and the argument is invalid for this reason. In general, if the conclusion of a categorical syllogism is not definitely shown in a diagram of the premisses, then the syllogism is invalid. With OOO-2, we can say that the premisses certainly make the conclusion **possible,** but we cannot say that given the premisses the conclusion is **necessary.** Unfortunately, "coming close" does not count, any more than a basketball game lost by one point counts as any less of a loss than a "blowout" by 30 or 40 points. In the one-point game, we can certainly say on behalf of the losing team that a win was possible right up to the last second, but in the end a loss is a loss. And an invalid argument, no matter how plausible the conclusion might seem, is still an invalid argument. It is invalid precisely because of our original definition of invalidity: **it is possible for all the premisses to be true and the conclusion false.**

To provide one final bit of practice on drawing Venn diagrams, let us take an argument stated in English, put it into standard form, name the mood and figure, draw a diagram, and then decide whether it is valid. The following argument is taken from the exercises at the end of section 3.6 on p. 64:

> Some children are not stupid, so, because all stupid people make mistakes, some children do not make mistakes.

Our first task is to put the argument into standard form. Recall that a categorical syllogism must consist of all standard-form categorical propositions. Thus we have a little work to do with the argument above. "Stupid" is not a class, but "stupid people" is. Further, "make mistakes" and "do not make mistakes" are not forms of the verb "to be," so they cannot serve as the copula of standard-form categorical propositions. This is easily taken care of, however, by considering the class of "people who make mistakes." We can then change "make mistakes" to "**are** people who make mistakes" and "do not make mistakes" to "**are not** people who make mistakes." Incorporating all of these changes, we now have:

> Some children are not stupid people, so, because all stupid people are people who make mistakes, some children are not people who make mistakes.

We now have all standard-form categorical propositions, and we note that there are three different classes mentioned (children, stupid people, and people who make mistakes) and that each class is mentioned in two of the propositions. The next task is to put the syllogism itself into standard form, and this means identifying the major and minor premisses and the conclusion. The key to this is, of course, to identify the conclusion first; this will tell us which terms are the major and minor terms. The word "because," as we noted in Chapter One, is a premiss-indicator. Since the word "because" immediately precedes "all stupid people are people who make mistakes," this must be one of the premisses. Which of the remaining statements is the other premiss and which is the conclusion? Well, we see the word "so," which is a conclusion indicator. Normally whatever follows "so" would be the conclusion, but as it happens here the premiss which is indicated by the word "because" is inserted between "so" and the conclusion, with appropriate commas to avoid confusion. The conclusion then follows this premiss and is "some children are not people who make mistakes." When we think about it, we realize that this is rather a common way of speaking in ordinary language. It would be similar to saying, "All humans are mortal, so, because Socrates is human, he is mortal." The conclusion here is clearly "Socrates is mortal," the indicator is "so," and one of the premisses with its own indicator is inserted between "so" and the conclusion.

So we now know what one premiss and the conclusion are; the other premiss must then be "some children are not stupid people." We also know that when we put our syllogism in standard form we will list the two premisses first and then the conclusion. But which of the two premisses comes first? It will be the premiss containing the major term, and the major term by definition is the predicate term of the conclusion, "people who make mistakes." So the major premiss, which contains the major term and is listed first, will be "All stupid people are people who make mistakes." The minor premiss, listed second, will contain the minor term which is the subject term of the conclusion, "children." So the minor premiss is "some children are not stupid people." Thus the syllogism stated in standard form is the following:

> All stupid people are people who make mistakes.
> Some children are not stupid people.
> ∴ Some children are not people who make mistakes.

We can now easily name the mood and figure of the syllogism. The mood is AOO because these are the letters of the three categorical propositions in their proper order of major premiss, minor premiss, and conclusion. The figure is the first, because the middle term ("stupid people") appears in the subject term of the major premiss and the predicate term of the minor premiss. Our categorical syllogism, then is AOO-1.

We are now ready to test the syllogism for validity as we did with the examples above. We **could** label our circles with the actual terms of the argument, as long as we put the minor and major terms ("children" and "people who make mistakes") with the left and right circles respectively and the middle term ("stupid people") with the lower circle. **Or,** we could simply write out the form of AOO-1 using the letters S, P and M, and label the circles as we have been doing. If we use the latter way, we would first write out the form of syllogism AOO-1:

> All M are P.
> Some S are not M.
> ∴ Some S are not P.

Since our premisses are both a universal and a particular, we must, as above, diagram the universal one first. We will thus shade the "lower" part of the M circle, the entire part of it which lies outside the P circle. Our diagram now says "All M are P." For the minor premiss, "Some S are not M," we will draw an X in the part of the S circle which is outside the M circle. We notice a line (the P circle) going through the area where our X must go, so we put the X on the line to say that we do not know which side it is "really" on. The completed diagram then is the following:

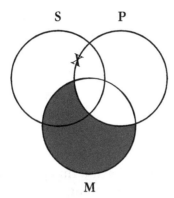

Figure 15

Now, is AOO-1 valid? The conclusion says, "Some S are not P." For this conclusion to be shown in the diagram, there would have to be a X in the S circle which at the same time is **not** in the P circle. Is this what we see? The X which appears in the diagram is in the S circle all right, but it is on a line such that while it **might** be in the P circle it also **might not** be in the P circle. Thus the conclusion is not **definitely** shown in the diagram; the best we can say is that given these premises the conclusion might be true. Since we cannot say that the conclusion is **necessarily** true, we have an invalid argument. And since AOO-1 is invalid, **any** argument in form AOO-1 is invalid. This would include the argument we have been testing which, as originally stated, read:

Some children are not stupid, so, because all stupid people make mistakes, some children do not make mistakes.

3.8 Testing Categorical Syllogisms For Validity: Aristotle's Way

We have just learned a way to take **any** standard-form categorical syllogism and test it for validity. We have also looked at some tips regarding the translating of "ordinary language" into standard form. A major question remains, however. Categorical logic has been presented above as having derived from Aristotle, a Greek philosopher of the fourth century B.C. Yet the method we have just learned is from John Venn, who lived in the nineteenth century A.D. How, then, did Aristotle himself and all the logicians in the 2300 years which separate him from John Venn, determine the validity of categorical syllogisms?

In what follows we will examine Aristotle's method, but in a modern presentation. It is customary to speak of Aristotle's "rules," a set of guidelines which must be met by any valid categorical syllogism. These "rules," tend to be worded and numbered differently in different logic textbooks, but the basic idea of each of them comes from Aristotle. We will discuss each rule in turn. To test any categorical syllogism by the rules, we simply ask whether it "breaks" any of them. If one or more rules is "broken," the syllogism is invalid. If no rules are "broken," the syllogism is valid. This is simply another way of saying that a valid categorical syllogism must meet all of the requirements for being valid; the rules are simply a convenient way of stating these requirements.

Rule 1: All of the terms in a valid categorical syllogism must have the same meaning each time they occur.

As we know, a categorical syllogism contains three terms referring to classes: the major, minor, and middle terms. Each term appears twice, and we normally presume that the terms have the same meaning in each occurrence. Consider the following syllogism, for example:

> Some calves are brown things.
> All calves are young cows.
> ∴ Some young cows are brown things.

The terms here are all straightforward, and we can easily show that the syllogism is in form IAI-3 and is valid. But what if someone tells us that, in the minor premiss, the word "calves" actually refers to the back part of the human leg between the knee and the ankle? We might question the sanity of anyone who would say such a thing, because then the minor premiss would be absurdly false, but still, we know that the truth or falsity of the premisses does not affect the validity of the argument. What has happened here is that the "middle term," is no longer **a** middle term at all, but in fact is **two** different terms. This means that the syllogism as a whole has four terms: young cows, brown things, "calves" meaning young cows, and "calves" meaning the back part of the human leg between the knee and the ankle. This is sometimes called the **Fallacy of Four Terms,** and we can now see that the syllogism is no longer a categorical syllogism at all since it has more than three terms. Of course, this same problem could occur with two or even all three terms of the syllogism—it is possible to have three terms each with two different meanings—but we use the expression "Fallacy of Four Terms" in any case. Note that this problem is not so much a problem with the logic of the syllogism as it is a problem of the syllogism not being in standard form in the first place.

Rule 2: The middle term of a valid categorical syllogism must be distributed in at least one of the premisses.

Recall our discussion of the distribution of the terms in the four categorical propositions. We distribute a term when we refer to every member of a class, and we do not distribute a term when we do not refer to every member of a class. Using the letters "d" and "u" for "distributed" and "undistributed" respectively, we summarize the four categorical propositions as follows:

$$A \;=\; \text{All } S^d \text{ are } P^u$$
$$E \;=\; \text{No } S^d \text{ are } P^d$$
$$I \;=\; \text{Some } S^u \text{ are } P^u$$
$$O \;=\; \text{Some } S^u \text{ are not } P^d$$

Now the middle term of a categorical syllogism, as we know, is the term which appears in both premisses. What Rule Two tells us is that the middle term must be distributed in at least one of its two appearances. If it is distributed both times, that is fine. But if it is not distributed in either of its two appearances, Rule Two is broken and the argument is invalid. Consider first a syllogism which does not break Rule 2, AAA-1:

All M are P.
All S are M.
∴ All S are P.

In the major premiss, All M are P, the middle term is the subject term of an A proposition. The subject term of an A proposition is always distributed, so the requirement expressed by Rule 2 is met. Of course, in the minor premiss the middle term is the predicate of an A proposition and is therefore undistributed, but this is fine since Rule 2 only requires it to be distributed in at least one premiss.

Now let us consider syllogism AAA-2:

All P are M.
All S are M.
∴ All S are P.

Here the middle term is the predicate of an A proposition in both of its appearances. It thus is undistributed both times, and the syllogism fails to meet the requirement of Rule 2. The syllogism is shown to be invalid for this reason, and it commits what we sometimes call the "**fallacy of the undistributed middle term.**" This squares with our finding earlier that the Venn diagram of AAA-2 showed the syllogism to be invalid.

It is important to reflect on why each of these rules is the way it is. Aristotle saw himself, not as laying down laws which all humans must follow when they reason, but rather as simply describing the way our reasoning actually works. In the case of Rule 2, we should consider the fact that the middle term is the one common element between the two premisses. Without the middle term, the premisses would be talking about completely different things. The middle term, to use a very rough and not-too-serious analogy, is like a friend whom two strangers have in common. The strangers may themselves become friends thanks to their common friend. Well, the conclusion of a syllogism is, in fact, a joint production of the major and minor terms. They **have** to get together in some fashion if there is to be a conclusion at all. So the middle term is crucial, but what does this have to do with its being distributed?

Think again of what it means to distribute a term: it means to talk about every member of that class. As long as the middle term is distributed once, every member of that class has been "covered," so to speak. This means that when the middle term appears in the **other** premiss, whether it is distributed there or not, the members of it mentioned there will be at least some of the same ones mentioned before. Consider AAA-1 once again:

> All M are P.
> All S are M.
> ∴ All S are P.

Since the M is distributed in the major premiss, then all members of M are said there to be members of P. This means that when M is mentioned in the minor premiss, even though it is undistributed there, these members of M will be among those which (according to the major premiss) are also members of P. And since the minor premiss says that all members of S are included in these certain members of M, the conclusion is necessarily that all members of S are members of P.

Let us make the point more concrete with a real argument:

> All dogs are animals.
> All collies are dogs.
> ∴ All collies are animals.

"Dogs" is of course the middle term. The major premiss distributes "dogs," so all dogs are said there to be members of the class of animals. This means that when dogs are mentioned in the minor premiss, even though the term is undistributed there, the ones mentioned there are among those which (according to the major premiss) are all animals. And since the minor premiss says that all collies are among this particular group of dogs, then we can conclude that necessarily all collies are included in the class of animals.

The same considerations show us why AAA-2 is invalid. Since its middle term is undistributed both times, there is no guarantee that **any** of the members of M mentioned in the major premiss are the same members of M mentioned in the minor premiss. Thus the two premisses might well have **no** members in common, even though they have the same middle term. This is illustrated by the following argument:

> All dogs are animals.
> All cats are animals.
> ∴ All cats are dogs.

Though the middle term, "animals," is mentioned in both premisses, it is obvious that those members of the class of animals referred to in the two premisses are two completely different parts of the class, namely those that are dogs in the major premiss and those that are cats in the minor premiss. So the premisses here have no members in common whatever, and no valid conclusion can be drawn from them. This, and not some arbitrary whim of Aristotle, is the reason we have Rule 2.

Rule 3: Any term which is distributed in the conclusion of a valid categorical syllogism must also be distributed in the premiss where that term appears.

The conclusion of any categorical syllogism which is in standard form will always contain the minor and major terms, in that order. Since the conclusion can be any of the four categorical propositions, either the major or minor term, or possibly both, might be distributed. Only when the conclusion is an I proposition can Rule 3 be dismissed, because in that case no term will be distributed in the conclusion. To see how Rule 3 works, let us begin yet again with our valid syllogism AAA-1:

> All M are P.
> All S are M.
> ∴ All S are P.

As we know, the A proposition distributes its subject term but not its predicate term. In the conclusion of AAA-1, then, the minor term S is distributed but the major term P is not. Rule 3 tells us that since S is distributed in the conclusion, it must also be distributed in the minor premiss where it first appeared. We can see that since S is, in fact, the subject term of an A proposition in the minor premiss, it is indeed distributed there. So Rule 3 is not broken, at least with the minor term. The major term P, of course, is not distributed in the conclusion. Rule 3 is concerned only with terms which are distributed in the conclusion, so it does not apply to the major term in AAA-1. It does not matter, in other words, whether the major term is distributed or not in the major premiss (it happens to not be distributed there). AAA-1, then, does not break Rule 3. Let's consider a syllogism which is not so fortunate, EAE-3:

> No M are P.
> All M are S.
> ∴ No S are P.

The conclusion is an E proposition, and thus distributes both terms. The major term P is also distributed in the major premiss as the predicate of an E proposition there, so it poses no problem. But look at the minor term S. In the minor premiss it is undistributed, because it is the predicate of an A proposition. Yet in the conclusion it is distributed, in violation of Rule 3. This mistake is sometimes called the **Fallacy of the Illicit Minor Term,** and the argument is invalid for this reason. Of course the same problem could happen with the major term, as in AOO-1:

All M are P.
Some S are not M.
∴ Some S are not P.

Here the minor term S is no problem since it is not distributed either in the conclusion or in the minor premiss. But the major term P is distributed in the conclusion as the predicate of an O proposition. Unfortunately, P is not distributed in its original appearance as the predicate of an A proposition in the major premiss. Thus AOO-1 commits what has been called the **Fallacy of the Illicit Major Term.** Whenever either the major or the minor term is distributed in the conclusion but not in its respective premiss, we will simply refer to such a syllogism as breaking Rule 3.

Now, why is Rule 3 so important? Think again of one of the basic requirements for **any** valid deductive argument, not just a categorical syllogism: the conclusion can never "go beyond" the premisses. The conclusion, in other words, can never encompass more information than what was already "contained" in the premisses. In a subtle way, a syllogism which breaks Rule 3 does just that. After all, if the conclusion of such a syllogism distributes a term which is not distributed in the premiss where that term first appeared, then the conclusion makes a statement about the **entire** class while the premiss only said something about **part** of that class. So the conclusion of such a syllogism really does "go beyond" or encompass more information than the premisses. To break Rule 3, then, is simply to fail to meet one of the basic requirements for any valid deductive argument.

An easy way to remember Rule 3, based upon this idea of the conclusion "going beyond" the premisses, is to think of your savings account. Think of the premisses as comparable to the deposits you make in your account and the conclusion as comparable to your withdrawals. You may withdraw an amount less than, or equal to, the total you have deposited in your account, but you may not withdraw an amount greater than the total of your deposits. Similarly, when you "withdraw" a conclusion from the premisses you have "deposited" in a deductive argument, you may not "withdraw" more information about a term than you have "deposited" in the premiss where that term was mentioned. Perhaps Rule 3 should have been called the **Fallacy of the Overdrawn Conclusion!**

Rule 4: The premisses of a valid categorical syllogism cannot both be negative.

This rule is simple and straightforward, yet devastating in its effect when we consider that it eliminates all the syllogisms which have premisses made up entirely of "E" and "O" propositions. Since the first two letters of the mood of each syllogism designate the premisses, this means that all syllogisms are ruled out which have moods whose first two letters are EE, EO, OE, or OO. How many syllogisms are affected? Consider: Each of these combinations could have a conclusion of any of the four categorical propositions. A mood beginning EE, for example, could conclude

EEA, EEE, EEI, or EEO. And of course, any of these moods could be present in any of the four figures. Mood EEA, for example, could be combined with the figures to produce syllogisms EEA-1, EEA-2, EEA-3, or EEA-4. The same is true for EEE, EEI, and EEO. So each of our four combinations of letters in the premises could be found with any of four conclusions, and each of these with any of the four figures. Each of the two-letter combinations, then, rules out **sixteen** of the categorical syllogisms. And since there are four such two-letter combinations, **sixty-four** categorical syllogisms are eliminated by Rule 4! This is one-fourth of the 256 categorical syllogisms. Of course, some of these will also break one or more of the other rules. OOO-3, for example, will fail to distribute its middle term (which will appear as the subject of an "O" proposition in both premises), and thus will break Rule 2 in addition to Rule 4.

To break Rule 4 is to commit what is sometimes called the **Fallacy of Exclusive Premises.** Why is this important? In a general way, we might say that the point of any categorical syllogism is to show some sort of relationship between the minor term S and the major term P. This relationship can be a negative one; it can say that certain S's are excluded from P. But at some point in the premises, something must be **affirmed.** At some point, in other words, we need information not just on what is **excluded** but on what is **included.** Otherwise, no conclusion can be drawn, because nothing has been said about the relationship between S and P. To make use of an admittedly rough analogy, consider two people who cannot agree on anything. Both are "negative," saying what they will **not** do. No agreement, not even an "agreement to disagree," can result from totally negative statements. (Of course, "negative" here does not mean the same thing as "negative" in the case of our categorical propositions—this is only a rough analogy.)

> **Rule 5: Any valid categorical syllogism with a negative premiss must have a negative conclusion, and any valid categorical syllogism with a negative conclusion must have a negative premiss.**

As with Rule 4, it is easy to see which syllogisms are ruled out here. They would be any syllogisms which have either an E or O premiss with either an A or I conclusion. Examples would be EAA, OII, AOI, IEA, etc. They would also include syllogisms with an E or O conclusion and both premises consisting of A or I propositions. Examples here would be AIO, AAE, IIO, IAE, etc. Of course, some syllogisms would break both Rules 4 and 5, e.g. EEI or OEA. These would have **two** negative premises (breaking Rule 4) with an affirmative conclusion (breaking Rule 5). To break Rule 5 is sometimes called the **Fallacy of Drawing an Affirmative Conclusion From a Negative Premiss,** though as we have seen, it can also involve drawing a negative conclusion from exclusively affirmative premises.

Rule 5 can be best understood by considering once again the nature of the categorical propositions. The affirmative one (A and I) tell us about S's being included in P, and the negative ones (E and O) tell us about S's being excluded from P. When an affirmative proposition is the conclusion of a categorical syllogism, it tells us about the inclusion of certain members of the minor term S in the major term P. In order to draw such a conclusion, both premises must have told us about what is included as well. If one of the premises tells us that something is **excluded** (as the negative propositions do), then that "chain of inclusion" consisting of minor term—middle term—major term cannot be completed. Similarly, if the conclusion is negative and thus tells us that certain S's are excluded from P, then at least one of the premises must also deal with what is excluded.

Rule 6: Any valid categorical syllogism with two universal premises must have a universal conclusion.

Once again, we can easily think of examples of syllogisms which would break this rule. Any syllogism with premises consisting exclusively of A or E propositions along with an I or O conclusion would do so, e.g. AAI, AEO, EAO, AEI, etc. When we think of the Venn diagram for such a syllogism, it becomes immediately obvious why the syllogism could not be valid. When we diagram universal propositions we use shading. When we diagram particular propositions we draw an X. Now if the premises are both universal, that means that our diagram will consist of two pieces of shading. Yet if the conclusion is particular, we will be looking for an X, and of course there will not be one there.

One would think that the opposite situation—two particular premises with a universal conclusion—would also break Rule 6. Strictly speaking, it doesn't, but such a syllogism would always be invalid for other reasons. To take one such example, IIA, Rule 2 would be broken since the middle term (appearing in two I propositions) could not be distributed even once.

It is worth noting in passing that one mood would break Rules 4, 5, and 6 simultaneously. This is mood EEI in any of the four figures. Consider: It breaks Rule 4 because it has two negative premises. It breaks Rule 5 because it has an affirmative conclusion with no affirmative premises. And it breaks Rule 6 because it has a particular conclusion with two universal premises. Syllogisms like this one which break more than one rule are, of course, no more invalid than those which break only one rule—there are no "degrees" of validity or invalidity—but rather are invalid for several different reasons.

Breaking Rule 6 is sometimes called committing the **Existential Fallacy.** We should note that this "rule" is a consequence of the proposal made by many modern logicians regarding the "problem of existential import" and its solution which was briefly discussed in section 3.4. Since we do not require members of the classes of universal propositions A and E to actually exist, we diagram these with shading only. Since we do require members of the classes of particular propositions I and O to exist, we diagram these by drawing an X to represent "at least one" member of the class. Though Aristotle himself would not have endorsed Rule 6 as above stated, he certainly was interested in the problem of existence and how we attribute qualities to things.

We have now looked at all six rules. To test any categorical syllogism by the rules is simple: we simply go through them one by one and ask whether the syllogism we are testing conforms to each of them. If one or more of the rules is broken, the syllogism is invalid; if no rules at all are broken, the syllogism is valid. Consider AAA-1 once again. We discussed earlier its conformity to the first three rules. Rules 4 and 5 would not be a problem since it has no negative propositions. Rule 6 would also not be broken, since its two universal premises are followed by a universal conclusion. AAA-1 is thus valid since it breaks no rules. This confirms our earlier Venn Diagram test of AAA-1 in which it was demonstrated to be valid. What we now have are two **independent tests** for any categorical syllogism. Any syllogism which has a Venn Diagram showing it to be valid will also conform to all the rules. Any syllogism which breaks one or more rules will have a Venn Diagram showing it to be invalid.

Exercises

I.   Listed below are the categorical syllogisms you put into standard form earlier. This time, in addition to putting them into standard form, draw a Venn Diagram for each and determine its validity or invalidity. For valid arguments, confirm that they are valid by showing that they break none of the rules. For invalid arguments, show which rule or rules they break. (Please note: None of these break Rule 1.)

1. Some students learn logic easily, because some students are capable of hard work and all those capable of hard work learn logic easily.

2. Some people who reason analytically are mathematicians, and because all logic students reason analytically, some logic students are mathematicians.

3. All collies are dogs, so some animals are collies, since all dogs are animals.

4. No computers have minds, for all people have minds and no computers are people.

5. Some children are not stupid, so, because all stupid people make mistakes, some children do not make mistakes.

6. No TV stars are "just plain folks," so some "just plain folks" are virtuous people, since some TV stars are virtuous people.

7. Some dogs are not cats, since some dogs are intelligent and no cats are intelligent.

II.   **Without** writing the syllogisms out, how can you tell that the following statements are true?

1. OEI-4 breaks Rules 4 and 5.

2. AAI-2 breaks Rule 6.

3. Any syllogism with an I conclusion can never break Rule 3.

4. Any syllogism with a mood beginning EE will never break Rule 2 but will always break Rule 4.

5. EEI in any figure breaks Rules 4, 5, and 6.

III.   Your turn! Take some mood/figure combinations of your own choosing. For each one, test it using both a Venn Diagram and the rules. Confirm that the two tests give the same result regarding the validity or invalidity of the syllogism. Keep going until you have at least one argument in each figure and at least one example of each of the rules 2–6.

3.9 Getting the Most Out of Categorical Logic

In the course of discussing categorical propositions and syllogisms, we have noted in passing that ordinary spoken and written language is far more varied than the rather strict "standard form" we require in logic. While we sometimes speak or write in exactly the words of "standard form," more often than not we vary our expression. Instead of "All dogs are animals," for example, we might well say any of the following: "Dogs are animals," "A dog is an animal," "Every dog is an animal," "Any dog is an animal," "Dogs are all animals," etc. Instead of "Some dogs are brown things," we might use any of the following expressions: "Some dogs are brown," "Lots of dogs are brown," "Many dogs are brown," "There are brown dogs," etc. Depending on the context, it would usually be reasonable and appropriate to "translate" any of the above expressions to the appropriate standard form proposition. In this section we will look briefly at a few other tips which will help us to move from ordinary language to categorical propositions. The more we can do this, the more applicable our work with categorical syllogisms will be.

There are many quantifiers in English besides "All," "No," and "Some." Several of these are mentioned in the paragraph above. Some of them are quite clear and obvious: "Every" clearly means the same thing as "All" and "Many" can be translated as "some" without any serious change in meaning. Others are not as clear: "A" and "The" can, depending on the context, be either universal or particular. "A dog is an animal" is clearly a universal statement which might appear in a child's book or a dictionary. It can easily be translated to "All dogs are animals." The same is true of "The dog is an animal." But what about "A dog is in my yard" or "The dog is in my yard"? It is just as clear that this is **not** a universal statement; it certainly does not mean that **all** dogs are in my yard. It refers, rather, to one dog, so we translate it as "Some dogs are things in my yard." It is not possible in our translation to distinguish between one, two, three, or several dogs being in my yard; all of these are uniformly represented with "some" since it means "at least one."

There is another important group of ordinary statements, those which begin with no quantifier but rather the name of an individual person or thing: "Socrates is mortal"; "That child is not behaving"; "This book has a red cover." Each of these statements (sometimes called **singular propositions**) refers to an individual, not to all members of a class and not to "at least one" member of a class. ("This book has a red cover" does not say that "at least one book" has a red cover; it says that **this** book I am now holding or looking at or talking about has a red cover.) So how do we translate such propositions? The conventional answer is based on the fact that classes can have any number of members from none at all to an indefinite number. There is nothing stopping us from discussing a class which has only **one** member, for example. We could call such a class a **unit class,** and we could say that all the members of this class have a certain characteristic. Of course, we understand that "all the members" means just one individual person or thing. It might sound awkward, but we can then translate "This book has a red cover" to "All 'thisbooks' are things with a red cover." We are saying here that the entire class of "thisbooks" (which consists entirely of **this** one book we are now discussing) are members of the class of "things with a red cover." So singular propositions can be translated as universal propositions about the unit class of which the thing being discussed is the only member. "This child is not behaving" would be a universal negative proposition: "No 'thischilds' are things that are behaving." "Socrates is mortal" would become "All 'Socrateses' are mortals."

Notice that we can now, at last, make it official that our "original" argument from Chapter One is valid. This was the argument dating from Aristotle himself:

> All humans are mortal.
> Socrates is human.
> ∴ Socrates is mortal.

We know that the first premiss can easily be translated to "All humans are mortals." But now we also know how to translate the second premiss and the conclusion: "All 'Socrateses' are humans" and "All 'Socrateses' are mortals" respectively. So now we have a standard-form categorical syllogism:

> All humans are mortals.
> All 'Socrateses' are humans.
> ∴ All 'Socrateses' are mortals.

The reason this argument is used as a model example of deductive reasoning is now clear. It is a categorical syllogism of form AAA-1 and has been shown valid by both the diagram and rule methods.

We have already referred to the fact that verbs other than "to be" can be handled with little difficulty. We simply use a form of "to be" and change the original verb to a noun or noun phrase. "Some people talk" becomes "Some people are talkers," and "All students work hard" becomes "All students are hard workers."

Syllogisms containing synonyms can simply be translated so that the same term is used throughout. Consider the following:

"All athletes are strong, because people who exercise are strong and all jocks work out."

With minimal effect on the meaning, we can change "work out" to "exercise" and "jocks" to "athletes." We add the quantifier "all" to "people who exercise are strong" since this seems to be making a universal statement. (Otherwise, it would have presumably said "some" or "many.") And of course we must change "strong" to "strong people." Finally, we put the whole thing in standard form:

> All people who exercise are strong people.
> All athletes are people who exercise.
> ∴ All athletes are strong people.

We see that it is of form AAA-1 and clearly valid.

Let us use some of the techniques we have just learned to have a little fun. You have probably heard of at least one version of this sort of "logical argument":

> God is good.
> Socrates is good.
> ∴ Socrates is God.

> The devil is bad.
> Hitler is bad.
> ∴ Hitler is the devil.

Variations on this kind of "argument" are often used to poke fun at logic—to show that "logic can prove anything." Well, the fact is that these arguments are invalid, and we can easily show this. Using the notion of a "unit class" as described above, we can translate the arguments as follows:

All "Gods" are good beings.
All "Socrateses" are good beings.
∴ All "Socrateses" are "Gods."

All "the devils" are bad beings.
All "Hitlers" are bad beings.
∴ All "Hitlers" are "the devils."

Both arguments are of the form AAA-2 and break Rule 2: the fallacy of the undistributed middle term. They are exactly like our earlier example of AAA-2:

All dogs are animals.
All cats are animals.
∴ All cats are dogs.

There are many other kinds of ordinary propositions which, with a little thought, can be translated into standard categorical form. Much of our ordinary, everyday reasoning can thus be put into the format of the categorical syllogism which allows us to test its validity and invalidity. Yet in this lengthy chapter we have only scratched the surface of Aristotle's contribution to the field of logic. Though we will soon see that other approaches have greatly expanded the logician's horizons, we will not lose sight of that basic building block of all human reasoning which Aristotle called the syllogism.

---CHAPTER FOUR---

Contemporary Logic

4.1 Why Classical Logic Has Not Been Rendered Obsolete

Most of the time when we hear about something "new," we think of it as replacing something "old." New cars, houses, unfortunately sometimes even friends, render the old ones out of date and make them candidates for the discard pile. As a way of living this is probably not one of our better ideas, but when it comes to the "new" and "old" approaches to logic it is positively wrongheaded. The recent developments in logic which date from the nineteenth but are primarily the product of the twentieth century are impressive indeed. They provide us with a way to deal with reasoning far more complex than the categorical proposition and syllogism. They provide the basic ideas behind much of contemporary computer theory. They provide a system of precise definitions and rules to help eliminate the ambiguities of ordinary language. They make complex processes much more simple and organized. For all of these reasons it is tempting to forget all about good old Aristotle and his categorical propositions and syllogisms, but we would be in a sorry state if we were to do this.

Modern "symbolic" or "truth-functional" logic as it is sometimes called, takes as its basic unit the individual or "simple" statement. Simple statements such as "Today is Monday" or "This is a logic book" cannot be broken down any further in symbolic logic. There is, in other words, no division into subject and predicate terms such as Aristotle has in his categorical logic. "Socrates is human" would have to be symbolized with one letter, e.g., "S" or perhaps "H." Thus we cannot readily discuss the internal logic of a syllogism such as:

> All humans are mortal.
> Socrates is human.
> ∴ Socrates is mortal.

It is because both Aristotle's logic and symbolic logic have their advantages that modern "quantification theory" has developed as a powerful attempt to combine the strengths of both. Although a detailed look at quantification theory is beyond the scope of this book, it will be discussed very briefly in Chapter Five. What we must do now, however, is to see what symbolic logic is and how it works.

4.2 Advantages of Constructing a Symbolic Language

Symbolic logic, as the name implies, involves the extensive use of symbols. What we will do, in fact, is to construct an **artificial symbolic language** which will have some things in common with ordinary spoken and written language. There are, however, several differences, and these differences are the advantages of our artificial language over ordinary language.

Clearly most of our reasoning is carried on through either spoken or written language. Whatever language we speak is a "natural" language which has evolved to its present state over a long period of time. All "natural" languages are full of ambiguities. Many terms have several meanings, and something said with one meaning intended might be heard with a quite different meaning. Punctuation marks—or tone of voice—can radically change what is being said. Colloquialisms develop so that what is perfectly obvious to one group of people is not at all clear to another—even though both groups speak the same language! Not surprisingly, therefore, communication **within** any one natural language—not to mention **between** or **among** different natural languages—is full of ambiguities and misunderstandings.

No one person invented natural language. Clearly all the real languages of the world evolved into their present state by being used and modified through countless generations. Our artificial symbolic language, however, was "invented" by a very small group of professional mathematicians and logicians in the past two centuries, and though it has several different versions, it is far more precise than any natural language. Terms and symbols mean what they are defined to mean. Though they are sometimes written differently by different logicians, expressions in this language come very close to universal acceptance regarding their meaning and use. Our artificial language of symbolic logic, then, is more like mathematics than it is like a "natural" language. This is a tremendous step toward removing the ambiguities inherent in natural languages.

Another distinct advantage of our artificial symbolic language can be seen by thinking once again of mathematics. We take our decimal-based system of arithmetic more or less for granted. But consider the state we would be in without it: Let us say that a Roman legion commander is about to go into battle against the barbarians, and he wants to know how many soldiers are at his immediate command. Fortunately, they are all standing in front of him in IX long columns, each column having LIX soldiers in it. Unfortunately, he has no obvious way of multiplying IX by LIX. Think of the advantage we have over him! A child can easily be taught to multiply 59 by 9. The difference is not in the problem being solved, but rather in the method through which this problem is symbolized. Roman numerals could not be multiplied in any simple way, though there are proposals regarding how the Romans may have made such calculations. Arabic numerals in the decimal system can, as we all learned in grade school, be multiplied in a very simple, straightforward manner.

4.3 Symbolic Logic as a Game

If the prospect of learning a new language appeals to you, great. Many people are less than thrilled about learning languages, however, and for this reason it might be useful to introduce a somewhat more appealing analogy. Learning symbolic logic is something like learning a new game. Think of a board game in particular, and imagine this scenario: You have just purchased a new board game which you have heard is fun, challenging, and perhaps even applicable to real-life situations. You open the box, and the first thing you do is to get a quick look at everything you find there: playing pieces, rules, the board, special cards or dice, etc. You then glance at the beginning of the rule book where a brief paragraph titled "Object of the Game" gives you an overview of what you'll be doing. Then you begin to learn about the different kinds of pieces and how they are used—the basic definitions and rules of the game. You go on to play the game, but at a rather elementary level. Soon you are playing the game at a higher, and then a still higher, level. You find yourself doing something which is fun, challenging, and perhaps even applicable to real-life situations.

4.4 Learning the Game: What Gets Symbolized?

Our game is called "Symbolic Logic" and we have just opened the box. From the title alone we know that something will be symbolized, that symbols will be used to stand for something. The question we are probably asking as we open the box, then, is "What gets symbolized in this game?" A quick look reveals that there are three kinds of symbols: symbols for **statements,** symbols for something called **statement variables,** and special symbols for something called **connectives.** Let us see what each of these kinds of symbols look like:

Symbols for statements

As we mentioned briefly above, the smallest "unit" in our symbolic system is the individual or "simple" statement, such as "This is a logic book," "Today is Friday," or "The weather outside is frightful." Each of these simple statements is symbolized using an ordinary capital (upper-case) letter. We choose a letter which will remind us of the statement, perhaps **L, F,** and **W** for the three statements just mentioned. Unlike categorical logic, we do not break statements down into subject and predicate classes.

Symbols for statement variables

Sometimes we will be talking about statements in general without referring to any particular statement. When we do this, we use small (lower-case) letters **p, q, r,** and sometimes **s.** Think of the way we refer in mathematics to just **any** number—we typically call it **"x."** If we want to talk about a relationship between two numbers such that one of them is always twice the other, we might well express it as **y = 2x.** Similarly, if we want to make the basic point that any statement must be either true or false, we might say, "A statement **p** must be either true or false." This refers to **any simple statement at all.** When we want to say something about the relationship between just **any two statements,** we use **p** and **q.** Any three statements would be **p, q, r,** etc.

Connectives

As just mentioned, we will often want to talk about relationships between or among simple statements. In ordinary English we put these simple statements together or "connect" them with such words as "and," "or," "if-then," etc. In our symbolic language there are five special symbols for connectives. Following our analogy of examining the entire contents of the game box right away, we will look briefly at all five of these symbols now, along with the names used for each of their logical operations. Following this we will take a much closer look at each of them individually.

1. **Conjunction:** The word "and" is normally used to **conjoin** or put together two statements. "Today is Monday and it is sunny," is an example of a conjunction. The symbol • is used to represent conjunction, so we might represent the above statement as **M • S.** If we want to represent the conjunction of just any two statements, we would say **p • q.**

2. **Disjunction:** We use the word "or," often together with "either," for the operation called **disjunction.** "Either today is Monday or it is sunny" would be an example. The symbol **v** represents disjunction, so we could say **M v S.** Referring to the disjunction of just **any** two statements, we would say **p v q.**

3. **Negation:** When we say that a given statement is not so, or not the case, this is called **negation.** The symbol ~ is written to the left of the statement we are negating. Thus, "It is not the case that today is Monday," or just "Today is not Monday" could be written ~**M.** The negation of just **any** statement would be ~**p.**

4. **Material Implication:** An "if-then" statement is called a **conditional** and the logical operation at work is called **material implication.** The symbol is written ⊃ and is called the "horseshoe." "If today is Monday, then it is sunny," could be written **M ⊃ S.** Just **any** "if-then" or conditional statement would be **p ⊃ q.**

5. **Material Equivalence:** Sometimes we want to say that two statements are equivalent to each other. As we shall see, there are several senses of

the word "equivalence," but let us consider a statement such as "Joe is a bachelor if and only if Joe is an unmarried man." What we are saying is that if Joe is an unmarried man then he is a bachelor, and if he is a bachelor then he is an unmarried man. In other words, if one is true the other is true, and if one is false the other is false. We use the symbol ≡, called a "biconditional," to say "if and only if." Thus the statement about Joe might be written **B** ≡ **U.** A statement saying that just **any** two statements are "materially equivalent" would be written **p** ≡ **q.**

4.5 Truth Tables: Conjunction, Disjunction, and Negation

If the previous section is comparable to opening the box of a new game and looking quickly at its contents, this section can be compared to looking at some of the game's basic rules for the use of its various pieces. Specifically we will look at the rules for conjunction, disjunction, and negation. Not surprisingly, the rules have been drawn from the way we actually use the terms "and," "or," and "not" in English, but just as in any other game the final authority for the use of these symbols will be the rules themselves, not any preconceived ideas we might have for what these terms **might** or **should** mean. Consider a parallel situation: The game of *Monopoly* is based on the way real estate transactions happen in real life: buying, selling, collecting and paying rent, improving property, paying taxes, etc. It is a rule in *Monopoly* that when you buy back a property you have mortgaged, you must pay 10% interest. This is roughly similar to real life, because when we pay on a mortgage we pay interest to a bank or other financial institution. In *Monopoly,* however, the interest rate is **always** 10%, is **always** paid in a "lump sum," is **always** due in full when a property is "bought back" or "unmortgaged," etc. We can argue about how similar or dissimilar this is to real life, but we **cannot** argue about the rule itself, since it is clearly stated among the rules of *Monopoly.* If it is *Monopoly* that we are playing, then this rule must be followed. The rules of symbolic logic are the same: We might argue about whether the rule governing, say, the "if-then" statement is really like the way we use such statements in real life, but we cannot argue about the rule itself so long as it is symbolic logic that we are doing.

Now, whenever we use any connective, we are dealing not merely with simple statements, but with compound ones. We need to take a moment to see what the difference is. Simple statements, stated by using individual capital letters as we noted above, contain no **other** statements within them. Simple statements can be short or long: "Today is Tuesday" and "Today is a beautifully sunny Tuesday in the month of July" are both simple statements. No other statements are "components" or "parts" of them. Like all statements, they are either true or false, and we can express this by saying that they have a "truth value" of either true or false. If the statement is true, then its truth value is "true"; if false, its truth value is "false."

Compound statements **do** contain at least one other statement as a "component" or "part" of them. All of the examples given above in explaining our various connectives are compound statements: "Today is Monday and it is sunny," "Either today is Monday or it is sunny," "It is not the case that today is Monday," "If today is Monday, then it is sunny," etc. In each case, one or more simple statements are contained within the compound statement. Consider "Today is Monday and it is sunny." The two simple statements are, or course, "Today is Monday" and "it is sunny." In the example of "It is not the case that today is Monday," the simple statement is "Today is Monday." The simple statement(s) contained within the compound statement are called "components" of it. Components must meet two requirements:

1. They must be simple statements in their own right.

2. They must be **replaceable** in the compound statement. This means that we must be able to remove them and replace them with just any other statement such that the new compound statement will at least make sense. For example, we could remove "Today is Monday" from "Either today is Monday or it is sunny" and replace it with, say, "Grass is green." The result would be "Either grass is green or it is sunny," which at least makes sense. so "Today is Monday" is a true component of the larger statement because it meets both requirements.

What would be an example of something which is **not** a component? Consider "The student with the red hair is short." The last five words in this statement **could** form a statement in their own right ("The red hair is short"), thus meeting the first requirement for a component. But the second requirement is not met, because we could not replace "the red hair is short" with just any other statement and have the result make sense. What if we try "Today is Monday," for example? We would then have "The student with today is Monday," which looks more like a computer glitch than a meaningful statement! Thus "the red hair is short" is not a component of the larger statement, and in fact "The student with the red hair is short" is a simple statement.

Every statement, whether simple or compound, has a truth value. As noted above, the truth value of a simple statement is either "true" or "false" depending upon whether the statement asserts something which really is true or false. What about the truth value of a compound statement? To answer this question we introduce a new term, truth-functional compound statement. **A truth-functional compound statement is a compound statement which has a truth value that is determined by (or is a function of) the truth values of its components.** Thus, "Today is Monday and it is sunny," is a truth-functional compound statement, because its truth value depends upon the truth values of its components, "Today is Monday" and "it is sunny." In addition to the truth value of its components, of course, the definition we give to the connective "and" will help to determine the truth value of "Today is Monday and it is sunny." The truth value of the compound statement will be affected according to whether the connective is "and," "or," "if-then," etc. In what follows we will see how the truth value of truth-functional compound statements is **completely** determined by (1) the truth values of their components, and (2) the definition of the connectives used in the statements. All of the compound statements which will concern us will be truth-functional ones.[1]

Conjunction

Let us look first at the logical operation known as **conjunction.** When we conjoin two statements with the word "and," we are saying that **both** of them are true. A conjunction, then, is true when both of its "conjuncts," as we call each component of it, are true. "Today is Monday and it is sunny," is true **only** when "Today is Monday" and "it is sunny" are both true. It is false if either or both of the conjuncts is false. To express this point in our symbolic language let us first take the statement and symbolize it. Since we use capital letters to represent simple statements, we can use **"M"** for "Today is Monday," and **"S"** for "it is sunny." Using our special symbol for conjunction, we can then say **M • S.** Now, to show the circumstances under which **M • S** can be true or false, we make use of a "truth table." As the name suggests, a truth table is simply a table consisting of T's and F's which stand for the truth values "true" and "false." We use such a table to show all the possible combinations of truth values which can occur for any given statement. We begin by listing T's and F's under each of the components of our conjunction (**M** and **S**) to show all of the possible combinations here. For two simple statements, each of which can either true or false, there are four combinations:

M	S
T	T
T	F
F	T
F	F

Now, adding the conjunction **M • S** to our table, and keeping in mind our point above about when it is true, we have the following:

---

[1] There are, in fact, compound statements which are not truth-functional. Consider the statement, "I think that he will come." The last three words, "he will come," fulfill both requirements of a component: they form a separate statement, and they are replaceable with just any other statement. Yet the truth value of "I think that he will come" is **not** determined by the truth value of "he will come." I might be wrong in what I think, or he might come even if I don't think he will. After all, logic is not psychology; there is not a logical way to determine when our thoughts about the world correctly correspond with the way the world really is. The only exception would be an omniscient being, i.e. God. For God, the statement "I think that he will come" would indeed be truth-functional; whatever God thinks is the case really is the case, since God knows everything. There is food for thought here; however we will not be concerned further about such statements. All the compound statements we will be considering from this point on will be truth-functional.

M	S	M • S
T	T	T
T	F	F
F	T	F
F	F	F

Let us review each line of the table. In the first line, today really **is** Monday and it really **is** sunny. The conjunction, "Today is Monday and it is sunny," is of course true. In the second line, today is still Monday but it is no longer sunny. The conjunction is now false because it says that **both** of these are true. In the third line, it is not Monday but it is sunny. Again, the conjunction which says that it is both is false. Finally, in the last line, it is not Monday and it is not sunny. Clearly, it is false to say that it is both. So a conjunction is true only where both conjuncts are true. Or to say the same thing another way, a conjunction is always false if either or both of its conjuncts is false.

Only one step remains to fully state the rule for conjunction. The truth table above shows when the particular conjunction **M • S** would be true and false. But now we want to say that the way this conjunction works is the way **any** conjunction works. To say this, we use statement variables **p** and **q** and we construct the following truth table:

p	q	p • q
T	T	T
T	F	F
F	T	F
F	F	F

This table is our definition of conjunction. It says that any conjunction is true **only** where both conjuncts are true.

Our connectives are always defined by truth tables. The meaning of conjunction, then, is completely expressed by the truth table above. The truth table, in turn, is derived from our ordinary usage of the term "and." There are many other terms in ordinary English (and of course countless terms in other languages) which often express conjunction. Some of the more common ones are: "but," "although," "nevertheless," "however," "whereas," "yet," "also," etc. Try each of these (and others you may think of) with our original example:

> Today is Monday, **yet** it is sunny.
> Today is Monday, **however** it is sunny.
> Today is Monday, **although** it is sunny, etc.

We might even add, "Today is Monday; it is sunny," using only a semicolon to indicate conjunction. There may be subtle differences among these, and perhaps different circumstances under which they might be used. However, they are all conjunctions because **the truth value is the same in all of them.** They are all true if both of their conjuncts are true, and false otherwise.

There are two interesting consequences of the way we have defined conjunction: (1) If we have a conjunction with one conjunct which is known to be false, the whole conjunction is false **regardless of the truth value of the other conjunct.** Thus a statement such as "Snow is green and there is life in outer space" is false, since we know that it is false that snow is green. We do not know whether it is true or false that there is life in outer space, but one way or the other, the conjunction is false since it has one false conjunct. (2) If we have a conjunction in which one conjunct is the direct negation of the other, the conjunction is false. Thus, "Snow is green and snow is not green" is false because the two conjuncts can never have the same truth value. If one is true, the other must be false and vice versa, since one is the direct negation of the other. In both of the cases just discussed, the "bottom line" is that it will never be possible to have the **one** thing needed for a true conjunction, namely, both conjuncts being true.

In addition to using words other than "and," we sometimes express conjunctions in ordinary language in an abbreviated way. Consider something like, "Jane is tall and Bob is tall." Symbolically we could write this as **J • B.** In English, however, we would probably abbreviate it to "Jane and Bob are tall."

Disjunction

We recall that what are commonly called "either-or" statements are referred to in symbolic logic as disjunctions. Here we have a bit more initial work to do than with conjunction, because there are two distinct kinds of "either-or" statements in English. We can call these two **exclusive** and **inclusive** disjunction:

Exclusive Disjunction: This form of disjunction is used when we make an "either-or" statement and mean to exclude the possibility of both alternatives being true. "You may have either soup or salad with your entree" is a statement often made by restaurant waiters, and this usually means that you may **not** have both, at least not without paying an extra charge. Exclusive disjunction, then, says "Either-or, but not both."

Inclusive Disjunction: This is the form of disjunction we use when we are considering two alternatives but do **not** mean to rule out the possibility of both being true. "I'll take either English or History next semester" would not usually be considered false if I end up taking both. Or to return to the restaurant, consider a buffet line where, for a fixed price, I can have whatever I want. Upon entering the buffet I remark to a friend that I will have chicken or steak. If I return to my table with either or even both of these on my plate, my friend will not be surprised. Only if I have **neither** of them on my plate might my friend remark that I must have changed my mind about having either chicken or steak. So inclusive disjunction says "Either-or, and possibly both."

Now as it turns out, our definition of disjunction in symbolic logic uses the **inclusive** sense of the term. (We will see why later.) We use the symbol **v** to stand for disjunction, so we could represent the statement, "Either I will have chicken or steak" as **C v S.** Our truth table for **C v S** would look like this:

C	S	C v S
T	T	T
T	F	T
F	T	T
F	F	F

This says that the statement is true whenever I have chicken, steak, or both chicken and steak (the first three lines). It is false where I have neither chicken nor steak (the fourth line). We call **C** and **S** the "disjuncts," just as the two simple statements making up a conjunction are called conjuncts.

To turn this table for the particular statement about chicken or steak into a general table defining just **any** disjunction, we simply change our labels and use statement variables **p** and **q.**

p	q	p v p
T	T	T
T	F	T
F	T	T
F	F	F

Based on this table, then, we can say that **any** disjunction is true when either or both of its disjuncts are true, and false when both disjuncts are false.

In ordinary language, we may express a disjunction in several different ways. "I will have either chicken or steak" could be expressed in any of these ways:

> "I'll have chicken or steak."
> "I will have chicken or I will have steak."
> "Either chicken or steak is what I'll have."
> etc.

Sometimes we use of word "unless" to express disjunction, as in "I will play baseball unless it rains." Notice, though, that the disjunction here is of the **exclusive** kind; what is being said is that either I will play baseball or it will rain, but not both. For now we can express this statement as **B v R,** but soon we will have a way of writing disjunction specifically in the exclusive sense.

As with conjunction, there are two interesting consequences of our truth table definition of disjunction: (1) If we have a disjunction in which one disjunct is known to be true, the whole disjunction will be true regardless of the truth value of the other disjunct. Thus, "Either snow is white or there is life in outer space" is a true statement because it is true that snow is white. We do not know whether it is true or false that there is life in outer space, but one way or the other, the disjunction is true because it has one true disjunct. (2) If one disjunct is the direct negation of the other, the disjunction is true. This is because the two disjuncts will have opposite truth values, and this means that one of them must be true. "Either snow is green or snow is not green" is true just as "Either snow is white or snow is not white" is true. Both (1) and (2) follow from the simple fact that the only thing which can make a disjunction false is **both disjuncts being false.**

Negation

We noted above that the symbol ~ is used to negate a statement. If **S** stands for "snow is white," then **~S** stands for "It is not the case that snow is white." This can be read in any of the following ways:

> "Snow is not white."
> "It is not so that snow is white."
> "The statement that snow is white is not true."
> etc.

The symbol simply reverses the truth value of whatever is to its immediate right. Thus, the truth table defining it is easy to produce:

$$
\begin{array}{cc}
p & \sim p \\
T & F \\
F & T
\end{array}
$$

We can look at negation as similar to a light switch (or a "toggle" switch for those more computer-literate). Whatever the condition of the light (whether on or off), throwing the switch once puts it in the opposite condition. Negation takes the truth value of the statement which it affects (whether true or false), and changes it to the opposite truth value.

So far, we have looked only at examples of the negation of simple statements, but compound statements can also be negated. To see how this is done, we must first look at how punctuation works in the language of symbolic logic.

4.6 Punctuation in Symbolic Logic

All languages, written and spoken, require punctuation. In spoken language we punctuate with looks, gestures, pauses, inflections, etc. In written languages some typical punctuation marks are periods, commas, parentheses, etc. Even in the language of mathematics—which in many ways resembles our artificial symbolic language—punctuation is necessary to avoid ambiguities. Consider the following simple arithmetic problem:

$$3 \times 7 - 2 = ?$$

Does this mean that we should multiply 3 by 7 and then subtract 2, getting 19 for an answer? Or does it mean that we should multiply 3 by 5 (the result of subtracting 2 from 7), getting 15 for an answer? In arithmetic there are several conventions regarding which operations take precedence over which, but perhaps the most common way is to simply use parentheses to indicate the operation which must be done separately. Thus, if we want an arithmetic student to multiply 3 by 7 and then subtract 2, we would write the problem as follows:

$$(3 \times 7) - 2 = ?$$

Here the answer is clearly 19. On the other hand, if we want the student to first subtract 2 from 7 and multiply 3 by the result, we would write the problem this way:

$$3 \times (7 - 2) = ?$$

And here the answer is definitely 15. The parentheses remove the ambiguity in the original problem. If we want yet another operation performed, say adding 6 to the final result, we can use brackets for the entire original problem:

$$[3 \times (7 - 2)] + 6 = ?$$

The order of solution is from "inside out," so we first subtract 2 from 7 getting 5, then multiply 3×5 to get 15, and finally add 6 to 15 for an answer of 21.

We have all worked through problems such as the above in grade school. The good news is that our symbolic language works the same way. Consider the following statement:

$$p \vee q \bullet r$$

Does this mean (1) the **disjunction** of either **p** or **q** • **r,** or does it mean (2) the **conjunction** of both **p v q** and **r?** Depending upon which we mean, we can use parentheses to make the desired statement:

p v (q • r) is (1) above.
(p v q) • r is (2) above.

To see that these really are different, consider the following example: "Bob is coming or Jean is coming and Mary is coming." This could mean either of the following:

(1) Either Bob is coming or both Jean and Mary are coming.
(2) Either Bob or Jean is coming, and Mary is coming.

Imagine you are planning a party and you receive these two messages. They say very different things! The first indicates that Bob may come alone, or instead of Bob coming at all, Jean and Mary may both come. The second says two things: first, either Bob or Jean is coming, and second, independently of this, Mary **is** coming. The first one is a disjunction in which the second disjunct is itself a conjunction. The second is a conjunction in which the first conjunct is itself a disjunction. Using the letters of the first names above, the two would be written symbolically as follows:

(1) B v (J • M)
(2) (B v J) • M

So, just as in math, parentheses are used in our symbolic language to remove ambiguities. They are used for the same purpose in English, along with our placement of "either," "both," commas and semicolons, etc. Brackets are used for larger expressions, as in this example:

[p v (q • r)] v p

This is a disjunction, where the first disjunct is (1) above, and the second disjunct is **p.**

There are several English expressions which we can now translate easily into our symbolic language. Consider a statement like "Neither Bob nor Jean is coming." This says that **both** Bob and Jean are not coming; Bob is not coming **and** Jean is not coming. We may write it in either of the following ways:

~(B v J)
~B • ~J

Recall that the negation sign reverses the truth value of whatever is immediately to its right. In the first formulation above, then, the negation sign reverses the truth value of the **entire expression in the parentheses.** In the second formulation, each negation sign reverses the truth value of the simple statement immediately following it. But **both** of these tell us that neither Bob nor Jean is coming.

Contrast this to "Bob and Jean are not both coming." This does not mean that one or the other will not come, but simply that they will not **both** come. If Bob is coming but Jean is not, it will still be true that they are not **both** coming. The same is true if Jean is coming and Bob is not. The statement, "Bob and Jean are not both coming," could be written in either of these ways:

$$\sim(B \bullet J)$$
$$\sim B \lor \sim J$$

The first says exactly what the English statement says: it is **not** the case that **both** Bob and Jean are coming. The second is logically equivalent to it: it says that either Bob will not come or Jean will not come. Soon we will be able to prove that these two formulations are logically equivalent to each other, as are the two formulations of "Neither Bob nor Jean is coming" above. However, the two **pairs** of formulations above are **not** equivalent to each other, just as "Neither Bob nor Jean is coming" is not equivalent in English to "Bob and Jean are not both coming."

We can now see how the exclusive sense of disjunction can be written in our symbolic language. Recall the example of "I will play baseball unless it rains," which we said can be looked at as an exclusive disjunction. It says that either I will play baseball or it will rain, but not both. Writing it as **B v R** seems inadequate, since our **v** symbol allows the possibility of both disjuncts being true. We can more accurately write the statement as follows:

$$(B \lor R) \bullet \sim(B \bullet R)$$

This says that either **B** or **R** but not both **B** and **R.** Using statement variables, we can say, then, that exclusive disjunctions can be written like this:

$$(p \lor q) \bullet \sim(p \bullet q)$$

Statements using the word "unless" are typical examples of exclusive disjunctions.

Exercises:

I.   Explain in a brief essay (one page at most) why the following statements are true. Refer to the truth tables for conjunction and disjunction in developing your essay.

   a.   A conjunction with one false conjunct is false.
   b.   A disjunction with one true disjunct is true.
   c.   A conjunction of any statement with its own negation is false.
   d.   A disjunction of any statement with its own negation is true.

II.   For simple statements, **"T," "F," and "U,"** assume that **T** is true, **F** is false, and **U** is a **single** statement of unknown truth value. What is the truth value (true, false, or unknown) of the following compound statements?

1. T v U

2. U • F

3. ~(U v F)

4. T • (F v U)

5. U v (T v U)

6. (F v U) • (U • F)

7. (T • U) v (F v U)

8. ~F v (T v U)

9. ~T • (F v U)

10. [U v (T v F)] • ~F

III. Using the suggested capital letters to represent each component of the statements below, translate the following into our symbolic language. When you have finished, make up some other statements and translate them!

1. Either Bob is not coming or both Jane and Zack are coming. **(B, J, Z)**

2. Neither Jean nor Dick is coming. **(J, D)**

3. Jane and either Bob or Dick are coming. **(J, B, D)**

4. Jane is not coming, but either Bob or Dick is coming. **(J, B, D)**

5. Dick and either Jane or Bob is coming, but Zack is not coming. **(D, J, B, Z)**

4.7 Material Implication and Its Truth Table

We come now to a type of statement known commonly as an "if-then" statement. It is also known as a **conditional** or **hypothetical** statement. The English word often used is "implies," and the logical operation is known as material implication. Though we are all familiar with such statements, there are many different kinds of them, as shown by these examples:

1. If all of the premisses of a valid argument are true, then its conclusion is true.
2. If this figure is a rectangle, then it has four sides.
3. If a heavy object is released in mid-air, then it will fall to the ground.
4. If you are good, then there will be something for you under the Christmas tree.

These statements are all conditionals because they all say that on the condition that one thing happens, something else will happen. The first part, following the word "if," is called the **antecedent** of the conditional. The second part, following the word "then," is called the **consequent** of the conditional. Before we examine what all conditionals have in common, let us look at what makes each of the four conditionals above different from the others.

The first one is what we might call the "logical" sense of "if-then." You recognize it from our earlier discussion of what a valid argument is. As a matter of logic, a valid argument is such that if all of its premises are true, then necessarily its conclusion must be true. For our first statement above to be false all of logic as it has been done so far would have to be rendered null and void.

The second statement is simply a matter of the definition of "rectangle." It must be true as long as "rectangle" means what it does. By definition, any figure which is a rectangle must have four sides.

The third statement is true as a matter of empirical observation. Due to gravity, releasing a heavy object in mid-air causes it to fall to the ground; we might call this a "cause-effect" or "causal" sense of "if-then." Since it is not a matter of logic or of definition, of course, we can certainly imagine something not falling, and in science fiction or dreams this sort of thing does happen (Superman flying, for example), but the observed fact is normally that heavy objects released in mid-air do fall to the ground.

The fourth example is a statement which is sometimes, but certainly not always, made by parents to children. Further, even though it is normally true, we can easily imagine circumstances under which it is false (the child is good, but the presents are stolen by the Grinch during the night, for example). The statement, in other words, is different from the others in that there is no logical necessity involved as in the first example, no question of a definition as in the second, no application of a scientific law as in the third.

What, then, do all four statements have in common? Once we answer this question we will know the root or basic meaning of material implication. Let us begin by comparing conditional statements to promises. Many promises are actually put in conditional form, "If so-and-so happens, then I will do such-and-such." But what is worth noting here is that the very nature of a promise is that we assume it will be kept. We would not take a promise seriously if we did not assume this. People break promises, of course, and no doubt the person being promised sometimes wonders about the promise being kept. But to the extent that we accept someone's promise and take it seriously at all, we assume that it will be kept. (Consider a promise to repay some money borrowed from a friend. Unless the friend doesn't care about the money and considers it a gift, he or she will loan it only upon hearing—and taking seriously—a promise to repay the debt.) Promises, to repeat, are normally assumed to be sincere, which is another way of saying that we assume they will be kept.

Conditional statements, in a similar way, are normally assumed to be true. We think of them as true unless something specific happens to make them false, rather in the way we assume promises will be kept unless they are definitely and clearly broken. Our question, then, becomes the following: Under what circumstances would we say that a conditional statement is false? To answer this, consider a very familiar situation. On the first day of class, the instructor hands the students a course syllabus and goes through the class policies and procedures to be sure everyone understands them. One of the stated policies reads as follows: "If the fire alarms sounds during a class session, class will be dismissed for the day." Let us state this symbolically, and to do this we must introduce the symbol $\supset$. Using **A** to stand for "The fire alarm sounds during a class session" and **D** for "Class will be dismissed for the day," we can state the above policy as the conditional **A $\supset$ D.** Now, let us ask under what circumstances **A $\supset$ D** is true and false. Since it is a stated course policy, it is like a promise; we would normally assume it to be true unless something specifically happens to show that it is false. Well, what could happen? Let us look at all the possible combinations of truth values for **A $\supset$ D,** keeping in mind that the question is what would have to happen specifically to make it false.

1. **A** and **D** might both be true. This would mean that at some point during the semester the fire alarm does indeed sound during a class session, and the instructor does indeed dismiss class for that day. Clearly the stated policy which was expressed in the conditional above is true.
2. **A** might be true and **D** false. This would mean that the fire alarm does sound during a class session, but the instructor does not dismiss class for that day. It is just as clear here that the stated policy was **not** followed; **A $\supset$ D** is false here.
3. **A** might be false and **D** true. This would mean that the fire alarm does not sound during a given class session, but class is dismissed for the day anyway. Does this violate the stated policy? No, of course not, because the policy never said that the **only** reason class might be dismissed would be for a fire alarm. Many other factors might cause a dismissal of class for the day: the instructor might feel ill, the material might all be covered early to the instructor's satisfaction, a special college program might be scheduled at that time, etc., etc. **A $\supset$ D** is still true, and this is perfectly compatible with—for example—**I $\supset$ D,** where **"I"** stands for "the instructor feels ill."
4. **A** and **D** might both be false. This would mean that the fire alarm never sounds, and class is never dismissed early. Think of how odd it would be in this case for a student, at the end of the semester, to say to the professor, "Well, I guess you didn't mean it about that fire alarm policy, right?" The answer would be that yes, the policy was indeed in

effect, but was never tested. **A ⊃ D** is indeed true in the sense that it was a stated course policy, but one might say in this case that the issue "never came up" since there was never a fire alarm.

Let us summarize the above discussion in the following truth table:

A	D	A ⊃ D
T	T	T
T	F	F
F	T	T
F	F	T

And let us then substitute statement variables **p** and **q** to expand our discussion from this particular conditional to **any** conditional:

p	q	p ⊃ q
T	T	T
T	F	F
F	T	T
F	F	T

The above table is our definition of material implication: **Any conditional statement is true except where the antecedent is true and the consequent false.**

Notice, now, that some rather odd things follow from this definition. For one thing, whenever the antecedent of the conditional is false, the conditional itself is true! The third and fourth lines of the truth table show this. This means that a false statement implies (in our basic meaning of "implies") any statement whatever. "George H.W. Bush was elected to a second term as president" (a false statement) implies **any** statement, e.g. "There is life in outer space," "Today is Tuesday," "Grass is green," "Grass is red," or whatever. Each of these statements is either true or false (though we do not always know which), so when any of them appears as the consequent of a conditional with a false antecedent, the situation in the third or fourth line will hold. And conditionals are true in either the third or fourth line. This "oddity" disappears when we consider that the word "implies" has the many different senses noted above, and that our definition of material implication merely captures what we might call the "common" sense of the term: conditionals are true except where the antecedent is true and the consequent false.

A second "oddity," which can be handled in the same way, is that if the consequent of a conditional is true, then the whole conditional is true. This means that a true statement ("Grass is green") is implied by any statement whatever! "There is life in outer space," implies that grass is green; "Today is Tuesday," implies that grass is green; "Today is not Tuesday" implies that grass is green, etc. But once again, there is nothing odd about this once we confirm from the truth table (which, after all, is the final authority) that in the first and third lines (the only lines in which the consequent is true) the conditional itself is always true.

Though conditionals are always written in the same way in symbolic logic, there are many different ways in which we might state them in ordinary English. As usual, a "natural" language (such as English) is much richer and has more variations—as well as ambiguities—than an artificial symbolic language such as the one we are learning. Take our conditional about the fire alarm again: **A ⊃ D,** where **"A"** stands for "The fire alarm sounds during a class session" and **"D"** for "Class will be dismissed for the day." While it would always be written symbolically as above, it could be **stated** in any of the following and numerous other ways:

> If the fire alarm sounds during a class session, class will be dismissed for the day (leaving out the word "then").

> Class will be dismissed for the day if the fire alarm sounds during a class session. (Antecedent and consequent are the same, but the order in which we state them is reversed.)

> The fire alarm sounding during a class session means class will be dismissed for the day.

> The fire alarm sounding implies that class will be dismissed for the day.

Notice that in every one of these cases (even the second one), the antecedent is "The fire alarm sounds during a class session" or some variation thereof, and the consequent is "Class will be dismissed for the day." We sometimes refer to the antecedent and consequent, respectively, as the "sufficient" and "necessary" conditions. The fire alarm sounding is a sufficient condition for class being dismissed for the day. Further, dismissing class is **necessary** if the fire alarm sounds—just ask a member of the class!

Exercises

I.   Explain in a brief essay (one page at most) why a false statement implies any statement at all. Discuss the definition of material implication in your essay.

II.   For simple statements, **"T," "F," and "U,"** assume that **T** is true, **F** is false, and **U** is a **single** statement of unknown truth value. What is the truth value (true, false, or unknown) of the following compound statements?

1. F ⊃ U

2. U ⊃ T

   3. U ⊃ U

   4. (U v T) ⊃ F

   5. T ⊃ (U • T)

   6. (U v F) ⊃ (U v F) (think twice about this one!)

   7. (U v F) • (U v F)

   8. [T • (U v F)] ⊃ T

   9. F ⊃ [(U • T) • T]

   10. (U v T) ⊃ (F • U)

III. Using the suggested capital letters to represent each component of the statements below, translate the following into our symbolic language. When you have finished, make up some other statements and translate them!

   1. Either we will play the game today or, if it rains, we will play tomorrow. **(P, R, T)**

   2. If it is raining then either it will clear up or the game will be canceled. **(R, C, G)**

   3. If we play the game, then either we win or we lose. **(G, W, L)**

   4. If we play the game and win, then we go on to the tournament. **(P, W, T)**

   5. If we play the game, then if we lose we do not go on to the tournament. **(P, L, T)**

4.8 Testing Arguments With Truth Tables

So far in this chapter we have been discussing statements and the various ways we connect simple statements together to form compound statements—conjunction, disjunction, etc. This is an important part of logic. Our **central** concern, however, is in learning to judge the correctness or incorrectness of logical **arguments.** We recall from Chapter One that an argument is a series of statements such that one of them (the conclusion) is said to follow from the others (the premises). In Chapter Three, we learned how to test the validity of the special kind of argument known as the Categorical Syllogism which, we recall, was made up of categorical propositions. Now we are ready to see how the statements or propositions of symbolic logic can be combined to make arguments, and then to see how these arguments can be tested for validity.

Let us continue the theme of the last set of exercises to construct two simple arguments. Stated in English first, they are:

(1):

> If we play the game, then we will win.
> We will win.
> Therefore, we play the game.

(2):

> If we play the game, then we will win.
> We play the game.
> Therefore, we will win.

Stated symbolically using the letters **P** and **W,** these same arguments are as follows:

(1)

$$P \supset W$$
$$W$$
$$\therefore P$$

(2)

$$P \supset W$$
$$P$$
$$\therefore W$$

You are on the right track if you suspect a problem with (1): there are other ways to win a game in addition to playing it. (The other team may not show up, or may have to forfeit for some reason.) You are also on the right track if you think that (2) is valid and a good piece of reasoning. In fact, (2) is indeed valid and (1) is invalid. Fortunately, however, we are beyond the point of having to rely on what "seems" or "looks" right to us; we are ready to **prove** conclusively that only (2) is a logically successful or valid argument.

The technique used to do this is to construct a truth table of the type we have been using earlier in this chapter. This time, however, instead of using a truth table merely to define a symbol, we will use it to **display all possible combinations of truth values for the premisses and conclusion of our argument.** Let us start with argument (1) above. We begin with columns for the two simple statements, **P** and **W,** and here, as earlier, we simply show all the combinations of truth values which can occur:

P   W
T   T
T   F
F   T
F   F

Now, to the right of these, we add columns for both premises and the conclusion of argument (1), labelling them as **P1, P2,** and **C:**

		P1	P2	C
P	W	P ⊃ W	W	P
T	T	T	T	T
T	F	F	F	T
F	T	T	T	F
F	F	T	F	F

Column **P1** is produced from our definition of the horseshoe. Columns **P2** and **C** are simply copied down from their original appearances on the left. (Soon we will avoid this duplication of the same column, but it is best to start with a full table which we can read very easily.)

This, then, is the truth table for argument (1). But what do we do with it? To answer this question, consider once again what the difference is between valid and invalid arguments: valid arguments are such that it is **impossible** for all their premises to be true at the same time their conclusion is false. Invalid arguments, by contrast, are such that it **is possible** for all their premises to be true and their conclusion false. Now look again at what a truth table is: it is a display of **all the possible combinations of truth values** for the statements it lists. This means that we can use a truth table to determine whether it **is or is not possible** for all the premises to be true at the same time the conclusion is false. If this **is** possible, the argument is invalid; if it is **not** possible, the argument is valid.

Each line of the truth table (reading horizontally or across) is a different possible combination of truth values. There are four possibilities in all. Look at the third line. In it **both** premises (all the premises there are in this argument) are true and the conclusion false. So **one** possibility in this argument is the very thing that **cannot** happen in a valid argument. **The third line shows that it is possible for all the premises to be true and the conclusion false, and thus the argument is proved to be invalid.** Of course the other lines show that it is also possible for both premises and the conclusion to be true (first line), for both premises to be false and the conclusion true (second line), and for the first premiss to be true while the second premiss and conclusion are false (fourth line). But since these combinations can occur in either a valid or an invalid argument, they do not determine the validity question one way or the other. The third line, on the other hand, **always** and **only** appears in an invalid argument, so it does determine that the argument we are considering is invalid. And note also that what we have shown is not that the argument is somehow one-fourth invalid and three-fourths valid, but rather that the **whole argument** is invalid because it contains the combination which appears in invalid arguments.

Let's look now at argument (2) above and see whether it is valid or invalid. Following the procedures just discussed, we produce the truth table for this argument:

		P1	P2	C
P	W	P ⊃ W	P	W
T	T	T	T	T
T	F	F	T	F
F	T	T	F	T
F	F	T	F	F

Look at each of the four lines (reading across). In the first line both premisses and the conclusion are true. In the second line, the first premiss and the conclusion are false while the second premiss is true. In the third line, the first premiss and the conclusion are true while the second premisses is false. In the fourth line, the first premiss is true while the second premiss and conclusion are both false. What is important here is what we did **not** find in our look at **all the possible combinations** of truth values for this argument. We did **not** find a combination in which all the premisses (that is, both premisses) were true and at the same time the conclusion false. Since this combination is not among the possibilities, we have proved that in this argument it is, indeed, **impossible** for both premisses to be true and the conclusion false. We have proved, in other words, that the argument is valid.

Argument (2), in fact, is an example of a rather well-known form called **modus ponens,** and this brings us to an important point which should be made before we look at further examples of truth tables. We know that arguments (1) and (2) above are made up of statements. **P** stood for "we play the game," and **W** stood for "we will win." But for every **argument** in our symbolic logic, there is a unique or **specific form** which corresponds to it. To discover the specific form of arguments (1) and (2), we substitute statement variables **p** and **q** for our statements **P** and **W.** We then have:

(1)

$$p \supset q$$
$$q$$
$$\therefore p$$

(2)

$$p \supset q$$
$$p$$
$$\therefore q$$

The truth tables for these would of course look just like those for the arguments themselves except for the labels at the top of the columns:

(1)

		P1	P2	C
p	q	p ⊃ q	q	p
T	T	T	T	T
T	F	F	F	T
F	T	T	T	F
F	F	T	F	F

(2)

		P1	P2	C
p	q	p ⊃ q	p	q
T	T	T	T	T
T	F	F	T	F
F	T	T	F	T
F	F	T	F	F

And thus the tables prove that these **argument forms** are invalid and valid respectively.

An **argument form** consists entirely of statement variables: **p, q, r, etc.** An **argument,** by contrast, consists entirely of statements: **A, B, C,** etc. **An argument form is the specific form of a given argument if that argument is produced when we substitute a different capital letter (simple statement) for each different statement variable in the argument form.** So argument form (1) above is the specific form of argument (1). The same can be said for argument form (2) and argument (2). Of course, there are countless arguments which might correspond to argument forms (1) and (2); we already mentioned that (2) is such a well-known argument form that it has been given a name, **modus ponens.** Each of these arguments which corresponds to a given argument form is called a "substitution instance" of that argument form, so argument (1) is a substitution instance of argument form (1) and argument (2) is a substitution instance of argument form (2). What, though, does it mean to say that any argument "corresponds" to a given argument form? It means simply that **when we take an argument form and substitute statements (capital letters) for state-**

ment variables (small letters), the resulting argument is a substitution instance of that argument form. These statements can be simple or compound, so a substitution instance of such an argument form as **modus ponens** can be an argument which "looks" just like **modus ponens** such as the following:

X ⊃ Y
X
∴ Y

But it can also "look" longer and more complicated, as in this example:

(A ∨ B) ⊃ ~D
A ∨ B
∴ ~D

In the first example above, statement **X** is substituted for **p** and statement **Y** is substituted for **q** in the form **modus ponens.** In the second example, statement **A ∨ B** is substituted for **p** and statement **~D** is substituted for **q. Both** of these are substitution instances of **modus ponens,** as are countless other arguments we might create. Note, however, that of the two examples above, **modus ponens** is the **specific form** only of the first one. If we substituted statement variables for each **simple statement** of the second one we would find that its specific form is the following:

(p ∨ q) ⊃ ~r
p ∨ q
∴ ~r

Why was it necessary to take time out from our look at truth tables to discuss the relationships among arguments, argument forms, specific forms, and substitution instances? It is because of the following very important relationship: **For any valid argument form, all of its substitution instances are valid arguments.** The opposite holds too: **For any invalid argument form, all of its substitution instances are invalid arguments.** Thus, when we said that argument forms (1) and (2) above were invalid and valid respectively, we automatically were showing that **any** substitution instance of (1) was invalid and **any** substitution instance of (2) was valid. Thus not only are our original **arguments** (1) and (2) (about playing and winning the game) proved invalid and valid respectively, but so are countless other arguments which are substitution instances of these forms. This is in keeping with one of the key characteristics of deductive logic, namely that validity is a function of form and not content.

Since the real "action" of deductive reasoning is to be found in **argument forms,** we will now look at several other such forms in order to become more confident about the truth table method. Consider the following one:

(p ⊃ q) v ~p
~ (p ⊃ q)
∴ ~p

Our truth table this time is a little more complicated. We will of course begin with columns for **p** and **q,** the statement variables. We will need columns for both premisses and the conclusion, but before we can produce these we need "helping" or auxiliary columns making up the individual parts of these statement forms. To see why, consider the first premiss:

(p ⊃ q) v ~p

This is a disjunction in which **p ⊃ q** is the first disjunct and **~p** is the second disjunct. Before we can determine the possible combinations of truth values for the whole disjunction, we need to know the possible combinations for the two disjuncts. Thus we will have "helping columns" for these, followed by our column for the first premiss (labelled **P1**). For the second premiss **(P2),** we can use our earlier helping column for **p ⊃ q** and simply negate it in each line. For the conclusion **(C),** we can simply label our helping column for **~p,** since this is also the conclusion. The result is the following truth table:

			C	P1	P2
p	q	p ⊃ q	~p	(p ⊃ q) v ~p	~(p ⊃ q)
T	T	T	F	T	F
T	F	F	F	F	T
F	T	T	T	T	F
F	F	T	T	T	F

If you prefer to "read across" from **P1,** to **P2,** to **C,** then you may always recopy the **~p** column at the right of the table, as we did with the **p** and **q** columns in our earlier truth tables. This is extra work, however, and in the table above we simply took advantage of the fact that **~p** is **both** a "helping column" **and** the conclusion.

What does the truth table show about the argument form we are considering? Keeping in mind that each horizontal row or line is a different possible combination of truth values, and that the four rows together constitute all the possible combinations that exist for this argument form, we consider each row in turn. **Only** if one or more rows show both premisses being true with the conclusion false will the argument be invalid; otherwise it will be valid. We can see that none of the rows shows the combination that would make the argument invalid. In each of the first two rows, one premiss is true and one is false while the conclusion is false. In both the third and fourth rows, the first premiss is true, the second premiss false, and the conclusion true. All of these combinations can occur in both valid and invalid argument forms, and the one combination which occurs **always** and **only** in invalid arguments—all premises true with conclusion false—does not appear. That combination is thus **impossible** in this argument form, and the argument form is therefore valid.

Let us now look at a few variations on the kinds of argument forms we have been considering. Some argument forms have only one premiss, as the following:

$$p \supset q$$
$$\therefore q$$

Since there is only one premiss, we can label it simply **P.** (Of course, there is nothing wrong with calling it **P1** as before.) The conclusion, **q,** is of course also one of our statement variables, so we might as well label the **q** column **C.** The table, then, is very simple:

		C		P
p	q		p $\supset$ q
T	T		T
T	F		F
F	T		T
F	F		T

We can see that the fourth row of this table makes the argument form invalid, for in this row the premiss is true and the conclusion false. Recall that an argument form is invalid if it is possible for **all the premisses** to be true at the same time the conclusion is false. Well, in this argument form, "all the premisses" means simply the one premiss we have. So it **is** possible for all the premisses to be true and the conclusion false, and thus the argument form is invalid.

Consider now the following argument form:

$$p \supset (q \supset r)$$
$$p \supset q$$
$$\therefore (p \supset r)$$

This time we have three statement variables **(p, q,** and **r)** rather than two. Since each of them can be either true or false, the addition of the third variable **r** means that more lines are needed in our truth table to show all the possible combinations of truth values. How many lines are needed? Consider: for each of the four lines in our previous tables, we now have the possibility of **r** being either true or false. Thus the four lines must be doubled to eight to express all these possibilities. Another way to look at it is that three variables, each with two truth values, would give us $2 \times 2 \times 2$ or 8 lines. Each additional statement variable would again double the number of lines in order for the table to show the possibilities: four variables would necessitate a table of sixteen lines, five would require 32 lines etc.

Now, how do we show these possibilities in a truth table? Let us first look at the table for just the three statement variables:

p	q	r
T	T	T
T	T	F
T	F	T
T	F	F
F	T	T
F	T	F
F	F	T
F	F	F

Notice that the vertical column for **r,** the third statement variable, reads **TFTFTFTF** from top to bottom. The next column to the left, the one for **q,** reads **TTFFTTFF,** and the column for **p** reads **TTTTFFFF.** This is the standard way of showing all eight possibilities and it is the way we will use throughout this discussion. Now, let us add the appropriate columns to complete the truth table for this argument form:

				P1	P2	C
p	q	r	(q ⊃ r)	p ⊃ (q ⊃ r)	p ⊃ q	p ⊃ r
T	T	T	T	T	T	T
T	T	F	F	F	T	F
T	F	T	T	T	F	T
T	F	F	T	T	F	F
F	T	T	T	T	T	T
F	T	F	F	T	T	T
F	F	T	T	T	T	T
F	F	F	T	T	T	T

We can see that there is no line of the eight in which both premisses are true and the conclusion false. Note that in the fourth line, one premiss is true, one false, and the conclusion false, but this is still a combination that can occur in both valid and invalid arguments. Since the combination of **all** premisses true and conclusion false does not occur, this means that such a combination is **impossible** in this argument form and thus the argument form is valid.

Let us consider one more argument form:

(p v q) ⊃ r
~p
∴ (r ⊃ p)

Following the techniques described above, we produce the following truth table:

				P1	P2	C
p	q	r	p v q	(p v q) ⊃ r	~p	r ⊃ p
T	T	T	T	T	F	T
T	T	F	T	F	F	T
T	F	T	T	T	F	T
T	F	F	T	F	F	T
F	T	T	T	T	T	F
F	T	F	T	F	T	T
F	F	T	F	T	T	F
F	F	F	F	T	T	T

Looking at each of the eight rows, we see that in two different rows, the fifth and seventh ones, both premises are true and the conclusion false. Thus there are two possibilities that an argument which is a substitution instance of this form might have all true premises and false conclusion. The argument form is thus invalid. (It is not, of course, any **more** invalid than our earlier ones which had only one such row; there are no degrees of invalidity.)

We have now seen that the truth table method enables us to take **any** argument form in our symbolic logic and test it. For each such argument form, our determination of its validity or invalidity is also a determination of the validity or invalidity of all arguments which are substitution instances of it.

Exercises

I.   Explain in a brief essay (one page maximum) **why** the use of truth tables allows us to determine the validity or invalidity of any argument in symbolic logic.

II.   Draw truth tables to show the validity or invalidity of the following argument forms:

1.

   p ⊃ q
   ∴ p

2.

   p ⊃ q
   p
   ∴ (q v r)

3.

   p ⊃ q
   q ⊃ r
   ∴ (p ⊃ r)

4.

   p ⊃ q
   ∴ q

5.

   p ⊃ q
   ~p
   ∴ ~q

6.

   p ⊃ q
   ~q
   ∴ p

7.

   p ⊃ q
   q ⊃ r
   ∴ (r ⊃ p)

8.

   p ⊃ (q v r)
   ~p
   ∴ (q v r)

9.

   (p ⊃ q) v (q ⊃ r)
   ∴ (p ⊃ q) • (q ⊃ r)

10.

   (p ⊃ q) • r
   q ⊃ r
   ∴ (p ⊃ r)

III. Consider the following argument:

If this logic course helps me to think more clearly, then I will be able to get a good job. This logic course helps me to think more clearly. Therefore, either I will be able to get a good job or I'm a monkey's uncle!

First, state this argument in our symbolic language, using the letters **C** for "this logic course helps me to think more clearly," **J** for "I will be able to get a good job," and **M** for "I'm a monkey's uncle!" Second, identify the argument form in Exercises II above of which this argument is a substitution instance. Third, tell whether this argument is valid or not **without drawing a new truth table.** Finally, state in a few lines how you were able to do this.

IV.   Make up at least one argument which is a substitution instance of each of the other argument forms in Exercises II above. State the argument in ordinary English **and** in the symbolic language using capital letters of your own choosing. **Without drawing a new truth table,** state whether each of your arguments is valid or invalid.

4.9 Tautologies, Contradictions, and Contingent Statements

We began this chapter by discussing simple and compound statements in our symbolic language. Then, in the section just completed, we put these statements together to form arguments, and learned how to test these arguments for validity using truth tables. Now, as the chapter draws to an end, we return to statements for a closer look.

Statements, by definition, are always either true or false. Of those that are true, some are **always** true and could not be false. "It is Monday or it is not Monday," symbolized as **M v ~M**, is such a statement. It is true because of its logical structure; specifically, it is a disjunction in which one disjunct is the negation of the other. Its truth table has all T's in the final column:

M	~M	M v ~M
T	F	T
F	T	T

Another example would be "If today is Monday, then today is Monday," symbolized as **M ⊃ M.** It too is true because of its logical structure; it is a conditional in which the antecedent and consequent are the same statement. Once again the truth table would have all T's in the final column:

M	M	M ⊃ M
T	T	T
F	F	T

Such statements are called **tautologies.** They have the following characteristics: (1) They are always true and could not be false. (2) They are true because of their logical structure, not their content; (3) Their truth tables will have all T's in the final column.

Just as some statements are always true, so some are always false. "It is Monday and it is not Monday" would be an example, where we agree that we are referring to the date **here** and **now.** We would symbolize this statement as **M • ~M.** This statement is false because of its logical structure; it is a conjunction of a statement with its own negation. The truth table for this and all such statements—called **self-contradictions**—will have all F's in the final column:

$$\begin{array}{ccc} M & \sim M & M \bullet \sim M \\ T & F & F \\ F & T & F \end{array}$$

Self-contradictions are, of course, the opposite of tautologies: (1) They are always false and could not be true; (2) They are false because of their logical structure, not their content; (3) Their truth tables will have all F's in the final column.

Thus far, we have dealt with statements which are either **logically true** (tautologies) or **logically false** (self-contradictions). The great majority of statements fall into the third classification, called **contingent** statements. Whether they are true or false is contingent or dependent upon circumstances in the world. "Today is Monday" is sometimes true and sometimes false, and this is a typical example of a contingent statement. It is the content and not the form which determines the truth value of a contingent statement; specifically it is the question of whether the real facts in the world correspond to what the statement claims the facts to be.[2] This means, of course, that the truth value of contingent statements is definitely **not** a matter of logic, which deals with form and not content. All logic can do is to note that contingent statements are sometimes true and sometimes false. Contingent statements are probably the most interesting of the three kinds, since they are the only ones that really give us information. Most of the examples we have given in defining our connectives have been contingent statements: "Today is Monday and it is sunny," "Either today is Monday or it is sunny," "If today is Monday then it is sunny," etc., symbolized respectively as

$$M \bullet S$$
$$M \vee S$$
$$M \supset S$$

What about the truth tables for contingent statements? As the above examples show, they will have a combination of T's and F's in their final column. We know

---

[2] As mentioned in Chapter One, the philosophical issues concerning the nature of truth, the world, and precisely what statements do are complex. In the present discussion of contingent statements, the "correspondence theory of truth" is presupposed; according to it, truth is found in the correspondence of our **statements** about the way we think the world is, on the one hand, to the way the world **actually is,** on the other hand.

from our earlier work in this chapter that the table for **M • S** reads, from top to bottom, **TFFF.** The table for **M v S** reads **TTTF,** and that for **M ⊃ S** reads **TFTT.**

Given, then, that all statements are either true or false, we have now seen all the possibilities. Any given statement is one and only one of the following:

1. A tautology: always true, table having all T's in final column;
2. A self-contradiction: always false, table having all F's in final column;
3. A contingent statement: sometimes true and sometimes false, table having a combination of T's and F's in final column.

All of the discussion so far in this section has been about statements, but we can now make a point parallel to our earlier discussion of arguments and their specific forms. Corresponding to every statement is a statement form which is the **specific form** of that statement. We can find the specific form of a given statement by substituting statement variables **p, q, r,** etc. for each simple statement. For our three contingent statements above, their specific forms are:

$$p • q$$
$$p \lor q$$
$$p \supset q$$

The tautologies we discussed, **M v ~M** and **M ⊃ M,** would have **p v ~p** and **p ⊃ p** as their specific forms respectively. The specific form of the self-contradiction **M • ~M** would be **p • ~p.** We can also say that for every statement form there are an unlimited number of **substitution instances** which result when we substitute statements (capital letters) for each simple statement variable in the form. Thus, **M v ~M** is a substitution instance of **p v ~p,** but so is the longer statement:

$$(A • B) \lor \sim (A • B).$$

In the first case, simple statement **M** was substituted for **p.** In the second case, compound statement **A • B** was substituted for **p.** Any substitution instance of a statement form which is a tautology will be a statement which is a tautology, so **(A • B) v ~(A • B)** is a tautology. Similarly, any substitution instance of a statement form which is a self-contradiction will be a statement which is a self-contradiction. Finally, any substitution instance of a statement form which is contingent will be a statement which is contingent.[3]

Sometimes it will not be obvious whether a given statement or statement form is a tautology, a self-contradiction, or contingent. Consider the following statement form:

---

[3] In most of what follows in this chapter we will be discussing statement forms rather than statements. We will often, for brevity's sake, simply use the term "statement." Keep in mind, though, that those expressions stated with small letters, **p, q,** and **r** are technically statement forms, which can have any number of actual statements as substitution instances.

$$[p \lor (q \bullet r)] \supset [(r \bullet q) \lor p]$$

This is a tautology, and if you look at it carefully you may see why. It is not necessary to "study" such a formula for clues as to its logical status, however. We may simply draw a truth table:

p q r	q • r	Antecedent p ∨ (q • r)	r • q	Consequent (r • q) ∨ p
T T T	T	T	T	T
T T F	F	T	F	T
T F T	F	T	F	T
T F F	F	T	F	T
F T T	T	T	T	T
F T F	F	F	F	F
F F T	F	F	F	F
F F F	F	F	F	F

Here we have all the "helping columns" needed to produce the antecedent and consequent of the statement form we are testing (which happens to be a conditional). Now we can produce the "final column" for the conditional itself:

$$[p \lor (q \bullet r)] \supset [(r \bullet q) \lor p]$$

T
T
T
T
T
T
T
T

We can see that the final column (which can always be placed to the right of the antecedent and consequent if we have enough room) has all T's. This shows that the statement form we are testing is **always** true and can **never** be false; thus it is a tautology.

Just as any argument or argument form can be tested for validity using a truth table, so any statement or statement form can be tested by truth table to see whether it is a tautology, self-contradiction, or contingent. The difference, of course, is that in testing an argument or argument form we produce columns in our truth table for all the premises and the conclusion, and then we look to see whether all the premises can be true in the same line where the conclusion is false. In testing the logical status of a statement or statement form, we produce helping columns as needed until we get the "final column" for the statement or statement form itself. Then we simply look at this final column to see whether we have all T's (tautology), all F's (self-contradiction), or some T's and some F's (contingent).

4.10 Material and Logical Equivalence

Earlier in this chapter we took a brief look at all five of the symbols for the "connectives" which put simple statements together to form compound ones. We have now worked extensively with four of these. The one we have so far ignored is the biconditional symbol ≡ for the operation called "material equivalence." This, you may recall, is the name for the relationship between statements which we express with the English phrase "if and only if." A statement containing this symbol is also a "biconditional."[4] Thus, "Joe is a bachelor if and only if Joe is an unmarried man" is a biconditional which could be symbolized as **B ≡ U.** We can think of a biconditional as a two-way conditional (hence the name); this one says that if Joe is a bachelor then he is an unmarried man **and** if he is an unmarried man then he is a bachelor. In other words, **B ≡ U** is equivalent to saying **(B ⊃ U) • (U ⊃ B).**

To see how the biconditional is defined by a truth table, consider the fact that its use is almost identical in symbolic logic to the use of the equal sign **(=)** in ordinary arithmetic. Pretend for a moment that you are a first grade teacher, and one of your students has handed you a set of arithmetic problems. You will mark these to show which ones are right and which are wrong. The problems are **equations,** though this term is not usually used in first grade. They all claim that some combination of numbers is equal to another number. Since these were done by a first grader who is just learning arithmetic, you naturally do not expect them all to be correct. Let us say your marking system is to put a T for "true" beside the correct problems and an F for "false" beside the ones which are missed. Here is the graded paper:

$$2 + 3 = 5 \quad \text{T}$$
$$7 - 4 = 2 \quad \text{F}$$
$$6 + 2 = 9 \quad \text{F}$$
$$6 - 4 = 2 \quad \text{T}$$

Your student is correct on the first and last equation, and incorrect on the second and third. Now, what was your criterion or standard when you marked the paper? Since they are all equations, they all claim that the numerical values on the two sides of the equal sign are the same. The first one, for example, claims that the numerical value of 2 + 3 is the same as the numerical value of 5. Since this is correct, the first

---

[4] Unless noted otherwise, the term "biconditional" will be used in what follows to refer to a statement or statement form containing the biconditional symbol.

equation is true; it is what teachers sometimes call a "math fact." The second equation claims that the numerical value of 7 − 4 is the same as the numerical value of 2. This is not correct, but since the equation says that these values **are** the same, the equation is false. The third equation is like the second; it is false since it says that 6 + 2 is the same numerically as 9 and this is not so. The fourth equation is true since it says that 6 − 4 is numerically the same as 2 and this really is the case. In other words, **the equal sign in common arithmetic always says that the numerical values on either side of it are the same as each other.**

The biconditional functions the same way in logic. Here we are concerned with truth values, not numerical values, and there are only two truth values, "true" and "false." Consider the biconditional **p ≡ q,** where p and q are any two statements. It says that **p** and **q** have the **same truth value,** and it will be true where they actually do have the same truth value. It will be false where they do not have the same truth value. The truth table for **p ≡ q,** then, will look like this:

p	q	p ≡ q
T	T	T
T	F	F
F	T	F
F	F	T

This is the table which defines the operation known as material equivalence. Notice that **p ≡ q** is true in the fourth line as well as the first. This is because, in both the first and fourth lines, **p** and **q** have the same truth value (both true in the first line and both false in the fourth line), and since **p ≡ q** says that they have the same truth value, it is true in both these lines. On the other hand, **p ≡ q** is false in the second and third lines because it says that **p** and **q** have the same truth value and clearly they do not.

All statements which are biconditionals, like all other statements, will fall into one of the three groups we discussed in Section 4.9. In other words, they will all be tautologies, or self-contradictions, or contingent statements. Consider the following biconditional: **(p ⊃ q) ≡ (~p v q).** Like any other statement, we can draw a truth table to see which of the three kinds it is:

		Left side		Right side	
p	q	p ⊃ q	~p	~p v q	(p ⊃ q) ≡ (~p v q)
T	T	T	F	T	T
T	F	F	F	F	T
F	T	T	T	T	T
F	F	T	T	T	T

Notice that we have labelled the two "sides," the statements on either side of the biconditional symbol. This helps us keep track when we get to the final column, where we have put a T in every line where the two sides have the same truth value. As it turns out, this means that there is a T in **every** line, and this biconditional turns out to be a tautology.

Now, biconditionals which are tautologies have a special status. Consider that **all** biconditionals **claim** that their two sides are equivalent to each other; they all **claim** to be tautologies. This is similar to saying that all arithmetic equations claim that the formulas on either side of the equal sign have the same numerical value; the child who handed in the four equations we examined above claimed (or at least hoped) that they all were correct. All biconditionals, to repeat, claim that their two sides are equivalent or have the same truth values; they claim to be tautologies. Obviously many biconditionals are not, in fact, tautologies, but some (including the one above) are. **Those biconditionals which are tautologies are called logical equivalences.** This means that the statements on each side of the biconditional symbol are logically equivalent to each other—just as 2 + 3 is numerically equivalent to 5. Logical equivalences, then, are a special group of material equivalences, namely the ones which are tautologies. The relationship between logical equivalences and all material equivalences is similar to the relationship between "correct" arithmetic equations and **all** the countless equations that could be written. An arithmetic book might contain a list of all the correct "math facts" from 1 to 10 (1 + 1 = 2, 1 + 2 = 3, etc.). Similarly, a logic book (such as this one) might contain a list of logically equivalent statements expressed as biconditionals. Sure enough, you will find such a list in the next chapter.

Exercises

I.   In a brief essay, explain what it means to say that all biconditionals claim to be tautologies but not all of them actually are tautologies.

II.   Draw truth tables to show whether the following statement forms are tautologies, self-contradictions, or contingent. For those that are biconditionals, state which of them are logical equivalences.

1. $(p \supset q) \bullet \sim(p \supset q)$

2. $(p \supset q) \bullet r$

3. $(p \supset q) \equiv (\sim q \supset \sim p)$

4. $(p \supset q) \supset (p \supset q)$

5. $[p \lor (q \bullet r)] \equiv [(p \bullet q) \lor (p \bullet r)]$

6. $[p \lor (q \bullet r)] \equiv [(p \lor q) \bullet (p \lor r)]$

7. $(p \supset q) \lor \sim(p \supset q)$

8. $(p \lor p) \supset \sim(q \lor q)$

9. $(p \supset q) \equiv (\sim q \lor p)$

10. $\sim(p \lor q) \equiv (\sim p \bullet \sim q)$

Formal Proof of the Validity of Arguments

5.1 How Truth Tables Can Get Complicated

In Chapter Four we learned that arguments in symbolic logic can be tested for validity using truth tables. This method, we recall, involves looking at all possible combinations of truth values for premises and conclusions to see whether the possibility exists of all the premises being true and the conclusion false. If such a possibility exists, it will of course appear on the truth table, and this will show that the argument is invalid. If such a possibility does not exist, a look at the truth table will reveal that this combination is not there, and the argument is valid since its conclusion must be true **if** all of its premises are true.

The truth table method can always be used in the above way, and the validity or invalidity of arguments can always be determined using it. Sometimes, though, arguments can consist of many premises (the longest ones we examined in Chapter Four had only two premises). Further, the premises themselves can be rather long and complicated statements. To whatever extent the argument gets complicated, the truth table also gets complicated; after all, we must have a column for **each** premiss, and often we must have one or more "helping columns" to produce our premiss columns. Consider the following argument:

"If I pass my logic course, I will get a good job. If I get a good job, then I will make money. I will pass my logic course. Therefore, either I will make money or the moon is made of green cheese!"

There is certainly nothing puzzling about this little argument. It is almost intuitively obvious that it is valid. If we use capital letters (P = I pass my logic course; J = I will get a good job; M = I will make money; G = The moon is made of green cheese), then we can state the argument symbolically as follows:

$P \supset J$
$J \supset M$
P
$\therefore M \lor G$

But consider the truth table we would have to draw to prove the validity of this argument. Since there are four different simple statements, the table would be sixteen lines long in order to express all the different truth value combinations. Then we would need columns for all the premises and the conclusion (we could label the **P** column as the third premiss and save a little work). Once all these columns are filled in, we would need to check each of the sixteen lines to see whether it ever happens that **all three** premises have T's at the same time the conclusion has an F. If we did all this, we would find that this combination never happens and the argument is therefore valid. But what a lot of work for a fairly intuitive argument!

Things can get much worse than the above situation. For every additional simple statement in an argument, the number of lines in the truth table is doubled. A fifth simple statement would require thirty-two lines, a sixth sixty-four lines, and so on. Further, the longer each premiss and the conclusion are, the more "helping columns" are needed. (There are no helping columns needed in the above argument.) In short, even though truth tables are the primary method to tell whether an argument is valid or invalid, we are left wishing for something a little easier in the case of arguments like the above in which the validity is fairly obvious.

5.2 Truth Tables and Formal Proof Compared

In this chapter we will introduce a method of formally proving the validity of valid arguments. This method solves some, but not all, of the problems alluded to above. For one thing, since the method involves proving **that an argument is valid,** it will not work with an argument which is invalid. If we have an argument which is not "given" to us as valid, using this method will not be appropriate. In other words, the truth table method is still what we must use when the question is, "Is this argument valid or invalid?" But when the question is, "How can I demonstrate or prove that this argument is, in fact, valid?" we can use the method of formal proof.

This is not as strange as it might sound at first. Consider what we do in geometry at the high school level, for example. We take theorems and prove that they follow from the axioms, definitions, and other theorems of Euclidean geometry. Our question is not, "Does this theorem follow or not?" but rather "How can I prove that this theorem does indeed follow?" The famous Pythagorean theorem, for instance, is presented to us to be proved—not to be questioned. There is (within the confines of Euclidean geometry) no question of **whether** the Pythagorean theorem is correct, but countless geometry students have expended their energies in showing **how** and **why** it is correct.

Another comparison might be to the sort of mystery story or play in which the outcome is known in advance, but where the interesting issue is **how** the detective will show this. Some episodes of the television show *Columbo* come to mind: Lt. Columbo knows "whodunnit" well in advance of the show's end, and so do we, but we are fascinated to see how he proves or demonstrates this. In short, it is not at all an idle exercise to construct a formal proof of something, even when we know that that thing is true.

In the method we are about to learn, the formal proof will be designed in each case to show that the conclusion of the argument in question does follow validly from the premises. As in geometry, the proof proceeds one step at a time; each step must be "justified" or backed up by referring to something we already know. Once a step has been justified, it can then be used as a justification for later steps. We will begin with the premises of the argument we are considering and show what follows from these, step by step. Our final step will be the conclusion of the argument.

5.3 The Rules of Inference and Substitution Instances

Keeping in mind Chapter Four's analogy comparing symbolic logic to a game, one always reaches the point where the best way to learn a new game is to simply start playing it. Let us, then, learn the method of formal proof by actually constructing a proof for the argument above. Our first step will be to restate the argument, and this time we will number each of the premises:

1. P ⊃ J
2. J ⊃ M
3. P / ∴ M v G

Notice that, in addition to numbering each premiss, we have moved the conclusion up to the same line as the third premiss. This is simply a convention in formal proofs; it does not change the third premiss **P**. The "/" symbol simply tells us that the premises are now finished. The conclusion, ∴ **M v G,** is then listed in the same line. This tells us what we must prove to follow from the premises. (One could just as easily say, "Prove that ∴ **M v G** follows from these three premises.")

Now, what do we do to actually construct the proof? The method is really very simple. It takes advantage of the point we emphasized in the last chapter regarding specific forms and substitution instances. Recall that we said that for any argument form that is valid, all substitution instances of that form will also be valid. Further, for any argument form that is invalid, all substitution instances of that form will be invalid. One of the argument forms we examined was called **modus ponens;** the name refers to the method of affirming something, and this is appropriate because this is what the argument form does:

p ⊃ q
p
∴ q

It begins with a conditional, **p ⊃ q.** Then it affirms that we have the antecedent of that conditional, **p.** From this, it follows that we have the consequent of the conditional, **q.** We proved that this argument form is valid using a truth table. This means that **without drawing a further truth table,** we know that any substitution instance of **modus ponens** will also be valid. Now look at the premisses of the argument we are discussing. Notice that the first and third premisses, **P ⊃ J** and **P,** exactly resemble the premisses of **modus ponens.** If we substitute **P** for **p** and **J** for **q,** we will have a substitution instance for the premisses of **modus ponens.** Thus from the first and third premisses of our argument, we can conclude **J,** since this is the conclusion of the substitution instance of **modus ponens** that we are considering, and since we know that **any** substitution instance of **modus ponens** is valid. **J,** then, follows from the premisses of our argument, specifically from the first and third premisses. We can list it as Step 4, and "justify" our step as follows:

1. P ⊃ J
2. J ⊃ M
3. P / ∴ M v G
4. J 1, 3, M.P.

The little note, **(1, 3, M.P.),** says that Step 4 follows from Steps 1 and 3 as the conclusion of an argument which is a substitution instance of **modus ponens.** In other words, Steps 1, 3, and 4 taken together comprise an argument which is a substitution instance of **modus ponens.** Once Step 4 is listed and "justified" as above, then it can be used as needed to justify further steps. It "joins" the original premisses as part of a "chain of reasoning" which will eventually lead us to **M v G,** the conclusion we are trying to prove.

What's next? Look again at the steps we have so far. Another substitution instance of **modus ponens** is found in Steps 2 and 4, **J ⊃ M** and **J.** When **J** and **M** are substituted for **p** and **q** respectively, Steps 2 and 4 are the premisses and **M** would be the conclusion of this substitution instance. We can thus list **M** as Step 5:

1. P ⊃ J
2. J ⊃ M
3. P / ∴ M v G
4. J 1, 3, M.P.
5. M 2, 4, M.P.

This time our "justification" note **(2, 4, M.P.)** says that **M** is the conclusion of an argument in which Steps 2 and 4 are the premisses, and which is a substitution instance of **modus ponens.** And once again, since **modus ponens** is valid, this new substitution instance is valid. We now have five steps to our argument—the three original premisses, and two further steps which "join" them since they follow validly as conclusions of substitution instances of a valid argument form, namely **modus ponens.** Each of the substitution instances is a little "mini-argument" within the larger argument.

Notice that since we now have **M** as a step in our argument, we have one disjunct of the disjunction **M v G** which is the conclusion we are trying to prove. Now it happens that there is another valid argument form which looks like this:

p
∴ p v q

This argument form goes by the name of **"Addition,"** and its validity can easily be shown by a truth table. (Try it if in doubt!) This means, of course, that any substitution instance of **Addition** will be a valid argument. If we substitute **M** and **G** for **p** and **q** respectively, we find that **M v G** follows from **M,** which was our Step 5. We can thus list **M v G** as Step 6.

1. P ⊃ J
2. J ⊃ M
3. P / ∴ M v G
4. J 1, 3, M.P.
5. M 2, 4, M.P.
6. M v G 5, Add.

The justification **(5, Add.)** says that **M v G** follows from **M** as the conclusion of an argument which is a substitution instance of **Addition.** Since **M v G** is the original conclusion we were trying to prove, we are now finished. In three additional steps beyond the original three premisses we have proved that **M v G** follows from those premisses by a series of steps, each of which follows from a step or steps which is either (1) an original premiss, or (2) something which itself followed from the original premisses. Contrast this to the sixteen-line truth table which would have been required to establish the validity of this argument—but keep in mind that the truth table would have shown **whether** the argument is valid or invalid while the method of formal proof simply provides a demonstration **that** the argument is, in fact, valid.

It will probably not yet be obvious how we were able to "come up with" the successive steps. What we hope is now clear is that each step, once shown to us, does indeed follow as its justification says it does. "Coming up with" the steps takes considerable practice, and toward this end some hints will be provided in the next section.

In the method of formal proof, there are nine basic valid argument forms which we will use. Every step of every proof (at this stage) can be justified as the conclusion of one of these nine argument forms, sometimes called "Rules of Inference." Here they are, along with the abbreviations we normally use in our justification lines:

Modus Ponens (M.P.)	Modus Tollens (M.T.)	Hypothetical Syllogism (H.S.)

$$p \supset q$$
$$p$$
$$\therefore q$$

$$p \supset q$$
$$\sim q$$
$$\therefore \sim p$$

$$p \supset q$$
$$q \supset r$$
$$\therefore p \supset r$$

Disjunctive Syllogism (D.S.)	Constructive Dilemma (C.D.)

$$p \vee q$$
$$\sim p$$
$$\therefore q$$

$$(p \supset q) \bullet (r \supset s)$$
$$p \vee r$$
$$\therefore q \vee s$$

Absorption (Abs.)	Simplification (Simp.)

$$p \supset q$$
$$\therefore p \supset (p \bullet q)$$

$$p \bullet q$$
$$\therefore p$$

Conjunction (Conj.)	Addition (Add.)

$$p$$
$$q$$
$$\therefore p \bullet q$$

$$p$$
$$\therefore p \vee q$$

Recall from the last chapter that substitution instances can be "one-to-one" substitutions of simple statements for statement variables as in the argument we just proved, but they can also be longer substitutions as in the following:

$$(A \vee B) \supset (X \bullet Y)$$
$$(X \bullet Y) \supset Z$$
$$\therefore (A \vee B) \supset Z$$

This is a substitution instance of **Hypothetical Syllogism,** when the following substitutions are made: **A v B** for **p, X • Y** for **q,** and **Z** for **r.**

---------------------------------- ❋ ----------------------------------

Exercises

I.   In a brief paragraph, explain how the method of formal proof is different from the truth table method when it comes to the validity of arguments.

II.   Each of the arguments below is a substitution instance of one of the nine Rules of Inference. Tell which it is in each case. (Hint: Eight of the nine rules are used once; one is used twice.) How do you know that all of these are valid?

1. R ⊃ (S • T)
    (S • T) ⊃ U
    ∴ R ⊃ U

2. D v (E ⊃ F)
    ~D
    ∴ E ⊃ F

3. [A ⊃ (B v C)] • (D ⊃ E)
    A v D
    ∴ [(B v C) v E]

4. B ⊃ (C v D)
    ~(C v D)
    ∴ ~B

5. A ⊃ B
    ∴ A ⊃ (A • B)

6. [J • (H v I)] ⊃ (K • L)
    [J • (H v I)]
    ∴ K • L

7. (A v B) • (C ⊃ D)
    ∴ A v B

8. Q
    ∴ Q v [R ⊃ (S v ~T)]

9. ~(A v B) ⊃ ~C
    ~(A v B)
    ∴ ~C

10. P ⊃ (Q v R)
    (S v ~T) v U
    ∴ [P ⊃ (Q v R)] • [(S v ~T) v U]

5.4 Putting Together Formal Proofs

Let us take another valid argument and demonstrate its validity, this time with a few hints on "coming up with" the steps:

1. (D v E) • F
2. ~D / ∴E

One good way to deal with an argument on first glance is to look at the conclusion. This tells us where we want to "go" with our proof. We want to show that **E** follows from these premises. Where does **E** appear in the premises? It appears in Step 1 as part of a disjunction which itself is the first conjunct of a conjunction. Now we notice that Step 2 is the negation of **D,** and further that **D** is the first disjunct of **D v E.** As we scan through the Rules of Inference, we notice that the argument form called **Disjunctive Syllogism (D.S.)** allows us to "eliminate" one disjunct of a disjunction. We could use **D.S.** on Steps 1 and 2 to conclude **E** except for one little problem: Step 1 doesn't **just** say **D v E;** it says **(D v E) • F.** This is a conjunction, not a disjunction, and **D.S.** will not produce a substitution instance for a conjunction. What can we do? We look over the Rules of Inference again, keeping an eye out for conjunctions. We find them in **Constructive Dilemma** (as the first premise), **Simplification** (as the only premiss), and **Conjunction** (as the conclusion). Of these, **Constructive Dilemma** does not have a form anything like the argument we are considering, and **Conjunction** moves from two simple statements to a conjunction. **Simplification,** on the other hand, goes **from** a conjunction **to** a simple statement which is the first conjunct. This is exactly what we need. We can take the conjunction which is Step 1 and "simplify" it so that we have only the first conjunct, **D v E.** This will give us the **disjunction** we need to use **Disjunctive Syllogism** to conclude **E.** The proof, then, goes as follows:

1. (D v E) • F
2. ~D / ∴E
3. D v E 1, Simp.
4. E 3, 2, D.S.

As you work through formal proofs—and the only way to become comfortable with this method is to **practice** it—you will find that patterns and connections will become more and more familiar to you. In the argument above, the fact that Step 1 is a conjunction and can thus be simplified may occur to you first. Or the Disjunctive Syllogism in Steps 3 and 2 may "jump out at you" before anything else. In the way we worked through the argument above, we reasoned "backwards" from the conclusion to what was needed to produce it, to what was first needed to produce **that,** etc. Of course, however we reason through the proof, the steps must ultimately be listed in an order such that each step follows from something before it. Since all of the Rules of Inference have either one or two premises, each step will always follow from either one or two earlier steps. Any substitution instance of Addition, Simplification, or Absorption will follow from a single step; substitution instances of any of the other six Rules of Inference will follow from two earlier steps.

Another thing to keep in mind is that, like geometry proofs or mysteries or puzzles, there will often be more than one way to formally prove the validity of an argument. Consider our original proof once again.

1. P ⊃ J
2. J ⊃ M
3. P / ∴ M v G
4. J 1, 3, M.P.
5. M 2, 4, M.P.
6. M v G 5, Add.

We proved the validity of this argument by showing two substitution instances of **modus ponens,** followed by an **Addition.** But a little examination will show that one could instead use a **Hypothetical Syllogism,** followed by one **modus ponens** and then the **Addition:**

1. P ⊃ J
2. J ⊃ M
3. P / ∴ M v G
4. P ⊃ M 1, 2, H.S.
5. M 4, 3, M.P.
6. M v G 5, Add.

Working through formal proofs can be fun in the same way that puzzles are fun. But like puzzles, proofs can sometimes be frustrating. If you get stumped on one, go on to another, or to something else altogether. The one that bothered you will always be there waiting—and probably will not be as difficult the second time around!

Exercises

I.   The first five of the following valid arguments can be proved to be valid with only **two** additional steps beyond the premises. The next five can be proved to be valid with **three** additional steps. Keep in mind, though, that in some cases other proofs with more steps—or perhaps even with the same number or fewer steps—can be constructed. Prove the validity of each argument using the method of formal proof.

1. A v C
    C ⊃ D
    ~A / ∴ D

2. J ⊃ K
    K ⊃ L
    ~L / ∴ ~J

3. D ⊃ (E v F)
    G
    D / ∴ (E v F) • G

4. J • (H v I) / ∴ J v H

5. (A ⊃ B) • (C ⊃ D)
    A / ∴ B v D

6. J • (K v L)
    J ⊃ (M • N) / ∴ M

7. (W v X) ⊃ (Y • Z)
    W / ∴ Y

8. M ⊃ N
    (M • N) ⊃ O
    M / ∴ O

9. D ⊃ (E v F)
    ~(E v F)
    ~D ⊃ G / ∴ G v E

10. A ⊃ B
    C ⊃ D
    A / ∴ B v D

II.   The following arguments are valid. Prove this by stating them in our symbolic language and then constructing a formal proof of the validity of each.

1. If I can learn logic then I can learn anything. Either the moon is made of green cheese or I can learn logic. The moon is not made of green cheese. Therefore I can learn anything.

2. If Bob comes to the meeting, then if Jane comes Ted will leave. If Jane does not come, we will cancel the election. Ted will not leave. Bob will come to the meeting. Therefore, we will cancel the election.

3. If Bob comes to the meeting, then Jane will come. If Mary comes to the meeting, then Ted will come. Either Bob or Mary will come to the meeting. Jane will not come. Therefore, Ted will come.

4. If I lose all my money on the lottery, then I can move in with my friends; and if I win the lottery, I can buy a mansion. If I move in with my friends, I will eat well. Therefore if I lose all my money on the lottery, I will eat well.

5. Either I will go crazy doing these proofs or, if I learn how to do them, I will be at peace with myself. I will not go crazy doing these proofs. I will learn how to do them. Therefore, I will be at peace with myself.

5.5 The Rule of Replacement and Its Role in Formal Proof

The nine Rules of Inference allow us to prove the validity of an enormous number of valid arguments in our symbolic language. Unfortunately, however, there are some arguments which are rather obviously valid and which cannot be proven so by the nine rules alone. Consider the following argument:

$$A \bullet B$$
$$B \supset C \; / \; \therefore C$$

It is obvious that C follows from these premisses. After all the first premiss says we have **both A** and **B,** and together with the second premiss we should be able to produce **C** with a **modus ponens.** Unfortunately, however, there is no rule by which we can isolate the **B** from the first premiss. **Simplification** allows us to take the first conjunct of a conjunction:

$$p \bullet q$$
$$\therefore p$$

But even though it is perfectly obvious that the second follows as well, the precise form of **Simplification** does not say this. This is frustrating, because we know very well that the order of the conjuncts in a conjunction makes no difference to the truth value (like a disjunction but **unlike** a conditional). We know, in other words, that **p • q** will always have the same truth value as **q • p.** We could even state this as a biconditional: **(p • q) ≡ (q •p).** The truth table for this biconditional would show it to be a tautology; thus we can say that **p • q** is **logically equivalent** to **q • p.** Recall our discussion of material and logical equivalence from Chapter Four. We said there that logically equivalent expressions are similar to numerically equivalent expressions. **2 + 3** is **numerically equivalent** to **5,** for example. But consider now what we can do in a math problem such as **(2 + 3) × 6 = ?** We can simply **replace** the

2 + 3 with **5,** since the two are numerically equivalent. Then we can go on to solve the problem: **5 × 6 = 30.**

Similarly, in our symbolic language, we can add to our original rules a **Rule of Replacement** which lists several logically equivalent expressions or tautologies, and tells us that we can replace any expression with one which is logically equivalent to it. Below is the usual list of these tautologies. These are not all the possible tautologies that could be constructed, but from this list and the original nine rules of inference we can prove the validity of any valid argument in our symbolic language:

> **The Rule of Replacement: Any expression in the symbolic language can replace any other expression which is logically equivalent to it.**

The following are logically equivalent expressions:

De Morgan's Theorems (De M.):	$\sim(p \cdot q) \equiv (\sim p \vee \sim q)$
	$\sim(p \vee q) \equiv (\sim p \cdot \sim q)$
Commutation (Com.):	$(p \cdot q) \equiv (q \cdot p)$
	$(p \vee q) \equiv (q \vee p)$
Association (Assoc.):	$[p \vee (q \vee r)] \equiv [(p \vee q) \vee r]$
	$[p \cdot (q \cdot r)] \equiv [(p \cdot q) \cdot r]$
Distribution (Dist.):	$[p \cdot (q \vee r)] \equiv [(p \cdot q) \vee (p \cdot r)]$
	$[p \vee (q \cdot r)] \equiv [(p \vee q) \cdot (p \vee r)]$
Transposition (Trans.):	$(p \supset q) \equiv (\sim q \supset \sim p)$
Material Implication (Impl.):	$(p \supset q) \equiv (\sim p \vee q)$
Material Equivalence (Equiv.):	$(p \equiv q) \equiv [(p \cdot q) \vee (\sim p \cdot \sim q)]$
	$(p \equiv q) \equiv [(p \supset q) \cdot (q \supset p)]$
Exportation (Exp.):	$[(p \cdot q) \supset r] \equiv [p \supset (q \supset r)]$
Tautology: (Taut.)	$p \equiv (p \vee p)$
	$p \equiv (p \cdot p)$
Double Negation (D.N.)	$p \equiv \sim\sim p$

This list, of course, is a list of **statement forms** which are logically equivalent to each other. But the same point made earlier about the relationship between argument forms and their substitution instances holds here as well: **Statements** which are substitution instances of logically equivalent **statement forms** are themselves logically equivalent and can thus replace each other wherever they occur. This means, to return to the example above, that **B • A** is logically equivalent to **A • B,** since this is a substitution instance of the logical equivalence listed above as **Commutation.** We can thus use the Rule of Replacement and complete the proof as follows:

1. A • B
2. B ⊃ C / ∴C
3. B • A 1, Com.
4. B 3, Simp.
5. C 2, 4, M.P.

There are some differences between our use of the Rule of Replacement and our use of the other rules. Since the first nine Rules of Inference are actually valid argument forms, each time we use them we are saying that an entire line of our proof follows from another entire line or lines as a substitution instance of one of these valid argument forms. With the Rule of Replacement we can also deal with entire lines: **~A v B** follows from **A ⊃ B** by **Material Implication,** for example. But in addition, we can replace **part** of a line with an equivalent expression. The statement **(~A v B) ⊃ C** can be replaced with **(A ⊃ B) ⊃ C,** because the antecedent of the first conditional is logically equivalent (by **Material Implication**) to the antecedent of the second conditional. Again we are reminded of simple arithmetic: **2 + 3** can be replaced by **5,** and this is true whether **2 + 3** is found as an expression all by itself, or whether it is part of a longer formula such as **(2 + 3) × 6 = ?**

The reason we can apply the Rule of Replacement in a wider way than the nine Rules of Inference, again, is simply that the Rule of Replacement does not deal with whole arguments but simply with logically equivalent expressions. In valid arguments, the whole conclusion follows from the whole premiss or premisses. Logically equivalent expressions, on the other hand, might be found wherever there are **any** logical expressions—and this of course can be in parts of statements, or in whole statements. It is important to keep this distinction in mind. We cannot, for example, take a statement like **(A • B) ⊃ C,** which is a conditional, and apply **Simplification** to its antecedent, getting **A ⊃ C.** If we should be tempted to do this, we must stop to reflect that **Simplification** is one of the Rules of Inference and thus applies to whole lines. It applies, specifically, to conjunctions and not to other statements which happen to contain conjunctions. By contrast, **A • (B ⊃ C) is** a conjunction, and thus it **can** be simplified to **A.** That is, **A** is a conclusion that we can draw from the premiss **A • (B ⊃ C).**

Another flexible feature of the Rule of Replacement is that expressions may replace each other "right to left" as well as "left to right." Take **Material Implication** as our example again. It says that **(p ⊃ q) is equivalent to (~p v q).** In the example above we replaced **~A v B** with **A ⊃ B,** and in doing so we moved from the expression on the right of the biconditional called **Material Implication** to the expression on the left. We can, of course, also move from "left to right" and replace **A ⊃ B** with **~A v B.** Since the two expressions are logically equivalent to each other, it makes no difference which replaces the other—just as it makes no difference in arithmetic whether we replace **2 + 3** with **5** or vice versa.

When we add the logical equivalences of the Rule of Replacement to our original nine Rules of Inference, we now have a means of proving the validity of all valid arguments in our basic symbolic language. Keep in mind, though, that if the question about a given argument is **whether** it is valid or invalid, the appropriate method to use is the truth table method. If the method of formal proof is tried on an invalid argument, the conclusion will never be reached.

Exercises

I. Explain in a brief paragraph **how** and **why** the use of the logical equivalences in the Rule of Replacement differs from the use of the first nine Rules of Inference.

II. Use the method of formal proof to show that the following arguments are valid. The Rule of Replacement will be needed along with the other Rules of Inference in each case. In some cases you will discover more than one way to prove that the argument is valid, but none of these arguments will require more than four steps beyond the premises.

1. A ⊃ (~B v C)
    (B ⊃ C) ⊃ D / ∴ A ⊃ D

2. J • (K • L) / ∴ K

3. C v ~~D
    ~C / ∴ D

4. (~K ⊃ ~L) ⊃ (M v M)
    L ⊃ K / ∴ M

5. (W v V) ⊃ ~(X v Y)
    W / ∴ ~X

6. X v (Y • Z)
    ~X / ∴ Z

7. C ⊃ D
    D ⊃ C / ∴ C ≡ D

8. A ⊃ ~(B v C)
    A / ∴ ~B

9. (J • K) ⊃ (L v M) / ∴ J ⊃ [K ⊃ (L v M)]

10. (A • B) v (A • C) / ∴ A

III.   The following arguments are valid. Prove this by stating them in our symbolic language and then constructing a formal proof of the validity of each. You will be using the Rule of Replacement along with the nine Rules of Inference.

1.   If John does not attend class, he will not pass the course. If he attends class, he will graduate. He will pass the course. Therefore, he will graduate.

2.   If either baseball or football is the national pastime, then labor problems will always be with us. Football is the national pastime. If labor problems will always be with us, then some games will be canceled. Therefore, some games will be canceled.

3.   If either Mary or Bob comes to the meeting then neither Jane nor Ted will come. Mary comes to the meeting. Therefore, Jane will not come.

4.   Either I will not learn logic or I will become a piano virtuoso. I will learn logic. Therefore, either I will become a piano virtuoso or I am a monkey's uncle.

5.   If either you or I win the lottery, then we will celebrate. We will not celebrate. Therefore you will not win the lottery.

5.6   Formal Proof and Invalid Arguments

We have seen that the method of formal proof can be used to demonstrate the validity of any valid argument in our symbolic language. What if an argument is known to be **invalid?** In this case, the method of formal proof must necessarily fail, since what it sets out to prove (the validity of the argument) is not the case. Consider the following **invalid** argument:

$$A \supset B / \therefore \sim A \supset \sim B$$

Using the method of formal proof, we can see that there are some statements that follow validly from the premiss of this argument. We might begin a proof in something like the following manner:

1. $A \supset B / \therefore \sim A \supset \sim B$
2. $\sim B \supset \sim A$ 1, Trans.
3. $\sim\sim A \supset \sim\sim B$ 1, D.N.

Any number of other steps could be tried, but no amount of work would ever give us the conclusion, **$\sim A \supset \sim B$.** This is very simply because this conclusion does not follow from the premiss, so no list of steps that **do** follow can ever include it. The invalidity of this argument can be shown by a truth table, of course, but one wonders whether there is a quicker way—comparable to the method of formal proof—to demonstrate the invalidity of arguments that are given to us as invalid.

There is such a way, and it is based simply on the definition of an invalid argument. An invalid argument is such that it is possible for all of its premisses to be true at the same time its conclusion is false. This is why truth tables work, of course—they show us whether this combination is possible or not. But with an argument known to be invalid, it is not necessary to look at the entire truth table to see whether such a combination exists. If the argument is invalid, such a combination **must** exist, and we need only to show that much. We need to show, in other words, that there is some set of truth values for **A** and **B** such that our premiss, **A ⊃ B,** will be true at the same time the conclusion, **~A ⊃ ~B,** is false. We can simply assign truth values to make this combination appear. Now both the premiss and the conclusion are conditionals, and we recall that a conditional is usually true. It is true, in fact, in every case except one, namely where the antecedent is true and the consequent false. So there will be many truth values for **A** and **B** that will make **A ⊃ B** true, but there will only be one combination that will make **~A ⊃ ~B** false. This would be the case where **A** is false and **B** is true, thus making **~A** true and **~B** false. That is the combination which would make our conclusion false, but would that same combination also make the premiss true? Yes, it would, because our premiss would then be a conditional with a false antecedent **(A)** and a true consequent **(B).** We have thus identified a possible set of truth values—**A** false and **B** true—which would make our argument's only premiss true and its conclusion false. The fact that there is such a combination shows that the argument is invalid. What we did, really, was to simply "go to" the line of the truth table which showed the invalidity of the argument. We did this since we knew in advance that there would be at least one such line, the argument having been presented to us as invalid.

The above argument was a rather simple one, having only one premiss. With a more complicated argument, the procedure is the same. Let us prove that the following argument is invalid:

$$(A \supset B) \bullet (C \supset D)$$
$$A \lor B / \therefore C \lor D$$

Notice that this argument looks at first glance something like a constructive dilemma, but a closer examination will show that C.D. will not work here. Neither will any other combination of steps get us to the conclusion, since the argument is known to be invalid. What we need to show is that there is a combination of truth values which will make **both** premisses true and the conclusion false. Look first at the conclusion. It is a disjunction, and the only way a disjunction can be false is if both its disjuncts are false. So we know that **C** and **D** must both be false in the combination we are looking for. What of **A** and **B?** They must have truth values such that both premisses will be true. Since the second premiss is a disjunction, we know that **A** and **B** cannot both be false, because otherwise the second premiss would be false. So either **A** or **B,** or perhaps both, must be true. Look now at the first premiss. It is a conjunction, and to be true both of its conjuncts must be true. The second conjunct, **C ⊃ D,** will be true since **C** and **D** are both false and a conditional with false antecedent and consequent is true. What of the first conjunct of our first premiss, **A ⊃ B?** It will be true with any set of truth values except **A** true and **B** false. But recall that we just said that either **A** or **B,** or perhaps both, must be true. This rules out the combination of both **A** and **B** being false, leaving two sets of values for **A** and **B** available: either they are both true, or **A** is false while **B** is true. This means that for the four simple statements in our argument, there are two possible combinations of truth values which would make both premisses true and the conclusion false:

A = True	or	A = False
B = True		B = True
C = False		C = False
D = False		D = False

If this sounds like considerably more work than our first example, reflect that the truth table proving the invalidity of this argument would have sixteen rows in order to display all the possible combinations of truth values for the four simple statements. What we just did was to immediately identify the two rows of those sixteen which would prove the argument to be invalid.

Exercises

I.   In a page or less, explain why the method of assigning truth values allows us to take a "shortcut" in proving the invalidity of invalid arguments. Why can this method not be used on valid arguments?

II.   Each of the following arguments is invalid. Assign truth values in such a way as to demonstrate the invalidity of each.

1. C ⊃ D
    D ⊃ E / ∴ E ⊃ C

2. J v K
    J / ∴ ~K

3. X ⊃ Y
    ~X / ∴ Y v Z

4. P • Q / ∴ (P • Q) ⊃ R

5. (J • K) ⊃ L
    L / ∴ J • K

5.7 Validity and Inconsistent Premises

An odd situation sometimes happens in an argument, and this is that we can know immediately that it is valid if its premisses are inconsistent with each other. Consider the following argument:

A v B
C
~C / ∴ D

This argument is valid, as a truth table would show. The table would have sixteen rows, of course, since there are four simple statements in the argument. An easier way to prove the argument valid is to construct a formal proof:

1. A v B
2. C
3. ~C / ∴ D
4. C v D 2, Add.
5. D 4, 3, D.S.

But a still easier way is to notice that the second and third premisses contradict each other. The premisses of the argument are thus inconsistent. What does this mean? Consider that the only way an argument can be invalid is for **all** of its premisses to be able to be true at the same time its conclusion is false. But this can never happen in the above argument or in any argument with inconsistent premisses. If **C** is true, then **~C** will be false, and vice-versa. The combination which **always** and **only** occurs in invalid arguments cannot occur, and thus the argument is valid. If we notice inconsistent premisses in any argument we know immediately that it is valid. (It can never be **sound,** of course, since this would require all of its premisses to actually be true.) Even if we do not notice the inconsistent premisses, such arguments tend to lend themselves to rather easy proofs as in the above case.

5.8 Quantification: Classical and Contemporary Logic Meet

In this final section of our chapter, we have a very modest goal. We will take a brief glance at the direction in which logic has moved in recent times as symbolic logic and "classical" logic have come together. What we have learned in Chapters Three, Four, and Five, is enough to enable us to take a very large number of arguments and prove them valid or invalid. It is enough, in other words, to not only give us a good look at the form and structure of logic but to give us the tools we need to apply logic to the "real world." With all of this, however, we have merely scratched the surface of the world of the contemporary logician. You have noticed that the kinds of arguments we dealt with in Chapter Three, involving categorical propositions and syllogisms, were quite different from those symbolic statements and arguments we covered in Chapters Four and Five. What exactly is the difference? Well, in Chapter Three we followed Aristotle's lead in examining the internal structure of the special kinds of statements called categorical propositions. We looked at the relationships between and among classes as we put these statements together into categorical syllogisms such as the following:

All dogs are animals.
All animals are living things.
∴ All dogs are living things.

By contrast, in Chapters Four and Five, we did not look into the internal structure of statements at all. We began with simple statements, put them together with each other to form compound statements, and then put these together to construct arguments which we then tested for validity. If we tried to test the above categorical syllogism using symbolic logic, we would fail. Each categorical proposition is a simple statement, and would thus have to be represented with a different capital letter. The argument, then, would look something like this:

D
A
∴ L

We can see what would happen if we tried to draw a truth table for this argument. There would definitely be a line in which both premises would be true and the conclusion false. The truth table, then, would prove the argument to be **invalid,** yet it is perfectly obvious that the above argument is valid. The problem, of course, is that symbolic logic is not designed to show internal relationships within statements; categorical logic is designed to do so, and we could easily show by a Venn Diagram that this argument is valid.

The branch of logic known as "Quantification Theory" combines the strengths of both earlier approaches. It allows us to look "into" a proposition and distinguish between individuals (such as Socrates) and the characteristics or attributes of these individuals (such as being human, being bald, etc.). It also allows us to distinguish between groups or classes (such as dogs) and their attributes (such as being animals, being quadrupeds, etc.). But in addition, it allows us to look at whole statements in their interconnections with each other. Let us look at these features.

Take a statement such as "Socrates is human." "Human" is a characteristic of the individual named Socrates. Our technique is to use a capital letter to designate attributes or characteristics, and a small letter to designate the individual having these characteristics. Thus we would use **"H"** to designate the characteristic of being human, and **"s"** to designate the individual Socrates. We write the attribute (capital letter) first, so we translate "Socrates is human" as **Hs.** Here are a few other examples:

Socrates is a philosopher   = Ps
Plato is a writer   = Wp
Europe is beautiful   = Be
Washington is our nation's capital = Cw

If we want to make a general statement about a whole group or class, we can make use of the letter **x,** which we call the "universal quantifier." We use it in the following way: Let us say we want to make the statement that all dogs are animals. We will say that for anything at all **(x),** if that thing is a dog, then it is an animal. This is a conditional statement, and we write it as follows:

$(x) (Dx \supset Ax)$

This can be read as: "For all x, if x is a dog, then x is an animal."

Let us say we want to make the statement that there actually exists a small dog. Here we make use of a new symbol, **∃x,** which is called the "existential quantifier." It says, "There exists something **x** such that . . ." So we can now say:

$(\exists x) (Dx \bullet Sx)$

This can be read as "There exists something **x** such that **x** is a dog and **x** is small."

Given the techniques of quantification theory, we can take arguments from categorical logic and translate them in such a way that we can indeed prove their validity using symbolic logic. Consider the argument above once again:

All dogs are animals.
All animals are living things.
∴ All dogs are living things.

As long as we represented each of these simple statements with individual capital letters, this argument looked to be invalid for the reasons we discussed. But let us try using quantification theory to represent each of these statements:

$(x) (Dx \supset Ax)$
$(x) (Ax \supset Lx)$
$∴ (x) (Dx \supset Lx)$

It is obvious now that the conclusion follows from the premises by Hypothetical Syllogism.

We can also use the existential and universal quantifiers to represent the propositions of the Square of Opposition. Let us take "dogs" and "animals" and state the four categorical propositions in the traditional way first:

All dogs are animals.   (A)
No dogs are animals.   (E)
Some dogs are animals.   (I)
Some dogs are not animals.   (O)

We can state these same propositions symbolically as follows:

(x) (Dx ⊃ Ax)   (A)
(x) (Dx ⊃ ~Ax)   (E)
(∃x) (Dx • Ax)   (I)
(∃x) (Dx • ~Ax)   (O)

A detailed treatment of quantification theory is beyond the scope of this book, but the above should be enough to show the great advance it represents. Using it, we can construct formal proofs of arguments which have lengthy compound statements as are found in symbolic logic, **and** which can have the internal structure of these statements examined carefully as in categorical logic.

Exercises:

I.   Explain in a paragraph or two why quantification theory represents an advance over both traditional categorical and symbolic logic.

II.   Translate the following statements using the notation of quantification theory. Use the existential and universal quantifiers as appropriate.

1.   Socrates is bald.

2.   All cats are frisky.

3.   There is a brown dog.

4.   Fido is cute.

5.   No logicians are neurosurgeons.

6.   Some cats are not loyal.

7.   Some cats are loyal.

8.   God is omnipotent.

9.   All gods are omnipotent.

10. Jane is late.

---------CHAPTER SIX---------

Some Further Considerations

6.1 The Applicability of Logic to Our Lives

In the beginning of this book we discussed the strengths and limitations of logic. We concentrated especially on the distinction between the **form** of our reasoning and its **content.** Logic (that is, deductive logic, which has been our primary emphasis) deals exclusively with the form of our reasoning. This is why logic alone cannot solve personal, moral, religious, or societal problems. Logic cannot tell me whether I should get married or not, whether I am allowed to lie to serve a greater good, whether there is a God, whether there will someday be peace on earth. Yet logic is essential in solving any of these and countless other problems, because we must be sure that whatever we conclude does indeed follow from the premisses we use. We must be sure, in other words, that our reasoning is valid. Otherwise, we run the risk of the conclusion being false even if all the premisses are true (the definition of an invalid argument). The goal in solving these or any other problems must always be **sound** reasoning, and we recall that this means that both the form and the content must be correct (the argument must be valid **and** all of its premisses must be true). Logic enables us to get the form correct—to produce valid arguments and reject invalid ones. Getting the content correct is the tricky part; we might say that life in general is a training ground in this skill. Here we are talking about education, life experience, age, maturity, expertise, and perhaps what the Greek philosophers called **wisdom.**

6.2 Why Mr. Data is Not the Captain of the *Enterprise*

Not everyone is a fan of the long-running *Star Trek* movies and multiple television series, but it is safe to assume that nearly everyone has heard of them and has given at least a moment's thought to some of the issues raised in the adventures of their many space-traveling crews. For some, of course, *Star Trek* is nearly a way of life, and for these folks the issues raised are thought-provoking and worthy of books, seminars, and heated discussions. From the beginning, *Star Trek* has raised and dramatized issues involving the nature of logic and its role in our lives. Mr. Spock, of course, was always referring to a certain course of action being "logical," even if such action did not intuitively "feel" right to Captain Kirk, Dr. McCoy and the others. Spock was half-Vulcan and half-human, and this juxtaposition of a purely "logical" Vulcan side with a somewhat vulnerable human side gave the character an appealing quality. The audience was encouraged to ask whether what is "logical" is always right or even sensible. Human emotion and pure logical deduction usually collided in situations involving Spock in his role as Science Officer.

It is in the second *Star Trek* crew, that of *Star Trek: The Next Generation,* that the nature and role of logic are confronted in an even more interesting and dramatically appealing way. The Science Officer of this crew is Mr. Data, and rather than being a mixture of a purely logical species with humanity, he is basically a logic machine. Mr. Data is an android, the creation of a brilliant scientist who merges a highly sophisticated computer with a human-looking and human-acting robot. All of Mr. Data's actions are responses to his programming, and these include not only the rapid calculations and analyses of data which are clearly the inspiration for his name, but also his human-like facial expressions and verbal responses in conversation. Like Mr. Spock, Mr. Data often speaks of human emotions, but unlike Spock who is half-human, Data can only speculate about what it might be like to feel love, anger, joy, sorrow, etc.

We have frequently compared the role and function of logic to that of a computer. The comparison is apt because a computer utilizes the same logical "paths" that we have learned. A computer is basically a vast array of circuits which are turned on and off. The two electrical "values" of any circuit are "on" and "off," just as the two truth values of any statement are "true" and "false." Just as we can construct truth tables for "and," "or," and other connectives, so in computers there are "and," "or," and other circuits. An "and" circuit is completed when two switches are turned on simultaneously, just as **p • q** is true when **both p** and **q** are true. An "or" circuit is completed when either or both of two switches is turned on, just as **p v q** is true when either or both of these disjuncts is true. Historically, the development of the computer is in part a result of the development of symbolic logic. Of course, a modern computer can do logical deduction at blinding speed, but the **kind** of thing it is doing is still the same **kind** of thing we have been learning in this book.[1]

Now, the *Enterprise* is fortunate indeed to have a Science Officer like Mr. Data. He brings to his job all the memory power of a state-of-the-art computer, and in addition he is constructed so as to physically perform such human tasks as giving and following orders, responding to questions, engaging in small talk, participating in policy making discussions, etc. Indeed, he is such an engaging "personality" that Captain Picard and his fellow crew members have a good deal of difficulty in remembering that he is not like them. In one episode it is proposed that Mr. Data be dismantled so that he can be studied with an eye toward making many more such androids. The philosophical

---

[1] My appreciation of the precise relation between logic and computers has been greatly enhanced through several conversations with my son Chris Gregory, an electrical engineer.

issues of what constitutes a person, whether androids are slaves, indeed whether Mr. Data is in a sense "human," are all confronted.

Why is Mr. Data not the Captain of the *Enterprise?* He is certainly more brilliant that Captain Picard, at least when we define brilliance in terms of memory, access to information, ability to see what logically follows in any situation, etc. What is it that Picard has over this computer-to-beat-all-computers?

To answer this question fully would go beyond the scope of this book. We can get some idea of the issues involved, however, by briefly looking at a debate which has occupied the attention of philosophers, scientists, computer designers, psychologists, and many other experts over the past half-century and more. This is the debate over "artificial intelligence" (AI), and there is heated controversy over the question of whether **any** artificial or man-made device can ever emulate humans in all our many activities. Clearly **some** human activities can not only be replicated in computers but can actually be improved upon, and these tend to be the ones which involve the logical skills we have learned in this book. Very simple computer programs can determine the validity of categorical syllogisms, for example. Somewhat more complicated programs can do truth tables (in which the values of "true" and "false" correspond to switches being turned "on" and "off," as noted above), and even formal proofs can be constructed by computers. All of these operations, and numerous more complicated ones, can be done more quickly and efficiently by computers than by humans. This is the sort of thing Mr. Data can do better than any human member of the *Enterprise* crew. So why isn't he the Captain?

Perhaps the answer lies in the fact that there are many other human mental operations beyond those which require logical processing skills. Not all experts believe that true "artificial intelligence" is possible. Most notable among the skeptics is Hubert L. Dreyfus, who for many years has argued that the human mind is not simply more complex than current computers in the kinds of operations it conducts, but actually **different in kind from any computer.** Dreyfus makes this point emphatically. Referring to the failings of recent research in AI, he says:

> . . . the basic point which has emerged is that **since intelligence must be situated it cannot be separated from the rest of human life** . . . If one thinks of the importance of the sensory-motor skills in the development of our ability to recognize and cope with objects, or of the role of needs and desires in structuring all social situations, or finally of the whole cultural background of human self-interpretation involved in our simply knowing how to pick out and use chairs, the idea that we can simply ignore this know-how while formalizing our intellectual understanding as a complex system of facts and rules is highly implausible.[2]

---

[2] Hubert L. Dreyfus, *What Computers Still Can't Do,* MIT Press, 1993, pp. 62–63. Emphasis is by Dreyfus.

Dreyfus even uses an example of a *Star Trek* episode from the original series:

> . . . the episode entitled "The Return of the Archons" tells of a wise states-man named Landru who programmed a computer to run a society. Unfor-tunately, he could give this computer only his abstract intelligence, not his concrete wisdom, so it turned the society into a rational plannified hell. No one stops to wonder how, without Landru's embodied skills, feelings, and concerns, the computer could understand everyday situations and so run a society at all.[3]

In the *Next Generation* series, it is probably fair to say that at least people do "wonder" about these things; the episode referred to above concerning Mr. Data's possible "personhood" would be an example. If Mr. Data is a "person" and **thinks** like a person, then Dreyfus is presumably wrong and there is no reason in principle why Data shouldn't be the Captain. If, on the other hand, Dreyfus is right, then we can enjoy *Star Trek* for the science fiction saga that it is. In this case, we should not expect **any** "logic machine" to perform human roles which require other skills in conjunc-tion with logic. Clearly the Captain of a Starship, along with the leader of a nation, the parent of a child, or the confidant of a friend, all require numerous human skills and capacities of which logic is merely one.

6.3 Why Mr. Data *is* Important to the *Enterprise*

Assuming we agree that Mr. Data should not be the Captain of the *Enterprise,* we can go to the opposite extreme and ask why he is important at all. Why, if he is not on a par with the human crew members, should we not replace him with a human Science Officer? Here the answer is more straightforward and less controver-sial. Whatever capacities Mr. Data may **not** have, it is clear what he **does** have, and that is the ability to manipulate information, process data, call on the resources of a vast memory, and engage in those deductive logical skills which we have studied in this book—and all of this with dazzling speed and accuracy. Add to this the fact that, unlike other computers, he is also an android built to at least simulate human words and actions, and his value to the Captain and crew is obvious. Similarly, we hope that it is obvious by now that logic's role in our lives is crucial and irreplaceable. No amount of common sense, insight, feeling, or intuition can replace good logical skills in living a human life, just as no amount of logical skill can replace common sense, insight, feeling, and intuition. All of the above are part of what it is to be human, and all are needed if we are to achieve a good life.

---

[3] Dreyfus, p. 63.

Glossary of Common Terms

Antecedent: The "if" part of a conditional statement; see material implication.

Argument: A series of statements such that one of them (the conclusion) is said to follow from the other(s) (the premises).

Biconditional: An "if-and-only-if" statement, true when the two statements making up the biconditional have the same truth value, false when they have different truth values. The symbol is "≡." The logical relationship present in a biconditional is called material equivalence.

Categorical Proposition: A statement about the relationship between two classes, in which the subject class (S) is said to be either included in or excluded from the predicate class (P), either totally (universal) or partially (particular).

Categorical Syllogism: A deductive argument consisting of three categorical propositions (two premises and a conclusion), in which two classes (major term and minor term) are said to be logically related to each other through a third class (middle term).

Class: A group or collection of things which have in common some quality or characteristic, e.g., "dogs," "logic books," "coins in my pocket now," etc.

Complement (of a class):   The class of everything which is not a member of the original class, e.g. "non-dogs" is the complement of "dogs."

Component (of a compound statement):   A part of a compound statement which (1) is a simple statement in its own right, and (2) can be replaced in the compound statement with any other simple statement such that the compound statement still makes sense. See Chapter Four.

Compound Statement: A statement which contains at least one simple statement as a component or part of it.

Conclusion: The statement in an argument which is said to follow from the premises.

Conditional: See "material implication."

Conjunction: An "and" statement, true when both of its parts or "conjuncts" are true; symbolized by "•." Also the logical operation present in such a statement.

Connectives: Words or symbols which "connect" or put together simple statements into longer compound statements—e.g. "and," "or," "if-then," etc.

Consequent: The "then" part of a conditional statement; see material implication.

Contingent Statement Form: A statement form which is neither logically true nor logically false, such as $p \supset q$; some of its substitution instances will be true and some false. The term can also refer to statements which are substitution instances of contingent statement forms, such as "If today is Monday, then I must go to work."

Contradictories: See square of opposition.

Contraries: See square of opposition.

Copula: The verb in a categorical proposition; always a form of "to be."

Deductive Argument: An argument in which the conclusion is claimed to follow necessarily from the premisses; always either valid or invalid. Also see inductive argument.

Disjunction: An "or" statement, true when either or both of its parts or "disjuncts" is true; symbolized by **"v."** Also the logical operation present in such a statement.

Distribute: To refer to every member of a class in a categorical proposition, e.g., "All dogs are animals," distributes the subject term, "dogs."

Figure: Any of four possible arrangements of the major, minor and middle terms in the premisses of a categorical syllogism.

Immediate Inference: An argument in which a conclusion can be directly drawn or inferred from one premiss.

Inductive Argument: An argument in which the conclusion is claimed to follow with some degree of probability from the premisses; always more or less probable but never necessary. Also see deductive argument.

Informal Fallacy: A mistake in reasoning which is due more to psychological than "formal" logical reasons. A discussion of several informal fallacies appears in Chapter Two.

Invalid Deductive Argument: A deductive argument with a form such that it is possible for all of its premisses to be true and its conclusion false. Only deductive arguments are valid or invalid.

Logical Equivalence: A biconditional which is a tautology, such as $p \equiv \sim\sim p$.

Major Premiss: The premiss of a categorical syllogism which contains the major term; listed first when the syllogism is put into standard form.

Major Term: The term in a categorical syllogism which appears in the predicate of the conclusion and in the major premiss.

Material Equivalence: The logical operation present in an "if-and-only-if" statement; see biconditional.

Material Implication: An "if-then" statement, true in all cases except when the antecedent ("if") is true and the consequent ("then") is false; symbolized by "⊃." Also known as a conditional. "Material implication" can also refer to the logical operation present in a conditional statement.

Middle Term: The term in a categorical syllogism which appears in both premisses.

Minor Premiss: The premiss of a categorical syllogism which contains the minor term; listed second when the syllogism is put into standard form.

Minor Term: The term in a categorical syllogism which appears in the subject of the conclusion and in the minor premiss.

Mood: A list of the letters designating, in order, the major premiss, minor premiss, and conclusion of a categorical syllogism.

Negation: A "not" statement, which always has the opposite truth value to that of the statement it negates; symbolized by "∼." Also the logical operation present in such a statement.

Performative Utterance: A sentence or expression which, when uttered in an appropriate context, performs an action, e.g.: "I promise you," "I apologize," etc.

Premiss: The statement(s) in an argument which are said to give evidence or reasons for the conclusion.

Proposition: See statement: these terms are used synonymously throughout the book.

Quality: In a categorical proposition, the characteristic of inclusion or exclusion of the subject class in (or from) the predicate class: always either affirmative or negative.

Quantifier: The word which indicates the quantity of a categorical proposition: "All" and "No" are the universal quantifiers and "Some" is the particular quantifier.

Quantity: In a categorical proposition, the number of members of the subject class said to be included in or excluded from the predicate class: always either universal or particular.

Rule of Replacement: In symbolic logic, the rule that allows any expression to be replaced with another expression which is logically equivalent to it. A list of logically equivalent expressions is given in Chapter Five.

Rules of Inference: Nine basic valid argument forms in symbolic logic, such as **modus ponens,** and **modus tollens.** Their use in the construction of formal proofs is discussed and summarized in Chapter Five.

Self-Contradiction: A logically false statement form such as **"p • ~p,"** false for all possible substitution instances. The term can also refer to statements which are substitution instances of self-contradictions, such as "It is Monday and it is not Monday."

Simple Statement: A statement which contains no other statements as components or parts of it, expressed in symbolic logic with a capital (upper-case) letter.

Sound Argument: A valid deductive argument which has all true premisses. Its conclusion is therefore true.

Specific Form: In symbolic logic, the form of any argument which is produced when a different capital letter (simple statement) is substituted for each different statement variable in the argument form.

Square of Opposition: A visual device which places the four categorical propositions in the four corners of a square, such that their logical relationships can be easily demonstrated. These relationships are: (1) Contradictories (A & O; E & I); (2) Contraries (A and E); (3) Subcontraries (I and O); (4) Subalternates (A & I; E & O).

Standard Form: The organization of a categorical syllogism when its parts are listed in the following order: major premiss, minor premiss, conclusion.

Statement: An assertion or claim that something is or is not so; always either true or false. Represented in symbolic logic by capital (upper case) letters. Also see: simple statement, compound statement, truth-functional compound statement.

Statement Variable: A symbol which can stand for just **any** statement rather than a particular statement. Small (lower case) letters **p, q, r,** etc. are statement variables.

Subalternates: See square of opposition.

Subcontraries: See square of opposition.

Substitution Instance: In symbolic logic, an argument which is produced when statements, either simple or compound, are substituted consistently for statement variables in an argument form; the resulting argument is a substitution instance of that argument form.

Tautology: A logically true statement form such as "**p v ~p,**" true for all possible substitution instances. The term can also refer to statements which are substitution instances of tautologies, such as "Either it will rain or it will not rain."

Truth-functional Compound Statement: A compound statement with a truth value which is totally a function of the truth values of its components, along with the definition of the connectives used.

Valid Deductive Argument: A deductive argument with a form such that, if all of its premises are true, then necessarily its conclusion must be true. Only deductive arguments are valid or invalid.

Venn Diagram: A visual representation, using circles, which can depict all four categorical propositions and also any categorical syllogism. Named after mathematician John Venn (1834–1923), the diagrams can be used to test the validity of categorical syllogisms.

Answers to Exercises in *Mind Your Logic*

p. 11:

I.   Logic can show us whether the form or structure of our reasoning is correct. It can show whether our conclusion follows from the premisses we use. It cannot show us whether the premisses or conclusion are, in fact, true. (Try this question again after the much fuller discussion of this point in Section 1.6!)

II.

1.   (a)

2.   (b)

3.   (c)

4.   (b)

5.   (d)

6.   (a)

7.   (d)

8.   (c)

9.   (b)

10. (a)

p. 22:

I.   Inductive and deductive arguments differ primarily in what they claim for their conclusions. Inductive arguments claim merely that their conclusions are probably true given the truth of their premisses, while deductive arguments claim that their conclusions are necessarily true, given the truth of their premisses. The distinction often mentioned as the difference between the two—regarding the move from specific to general statements (induction) and general to specific statements (deduction) does not cover all the cases of either kind of argument, and in addition does not describe the essential difference between the two.

II.

1. False

2. a

3. True

4. b

5. True

6. True

7. a

8. c

9. False

10. True

pp. 36–37:

I.

1. Petitio Principii

2. Argumentum ad Verecundiam

3. Division

4. Argumentum ad Hominem ("abusive" kind)

5. Amphiboly

6. Argumentum ad Misericordiam

7. Argumentum ad Baculum

8. Argumentum ad Hominem ("circumstantial" kind)

9. Converse Accident

10. Argumentum ad Populum

11. Argumentum ad Ignorantiam

12. Post Hoc

13. Equivocation

14. Composition

15. Accident

16. Converse Accident

17. Post Hoc

18. Black or White

19. Complex Question

20. Argumentum ad Verecundiam

21. Equivocation (or, perhaps, just a lighthearted play on words!)

22. Argumentum ad Populum

23. Complex Question

24. Argumentum ad Ignorantiam

25. Argumentum ad Ignorantiam

p. 44:

I.   Aristotle is the father of logic because he was the first to describe what is required for human reasoning to be correct. His discussions have become the basis for all future study of the form or structure of reasoning, as is evidenced by the present chapter. However, Aristotle was also the father of biology, of political science, of literary criticism, etc., so it is inadequate to think of him as "only" the father of logic.

II.   *Note: Other translations are possible, as long as the subject and predicate terms are <u>classes</u>. A noun or noun phrase is always needed.*

1.   Translate to "Some very small dogs are animals that bark loudly." Particular Affirmative (I) proposition; Subject class is "very small dogs" (undistributed); Predicate class is "animals that bark loudly" (undistributed).

2.   Translate to "All members of the history class are people who are in the classroom." Universal Affirmative (A) proposition; Subject class is "members of the history class" (distributed); Predicate class is "people who are in the classroom" (undistributed).

3. Translate to "No students with scores under 60 are people who passed the exam." Universal Negative (E) proposition. Subject class is "students with scores under 60" (distributed); Predicate class is "people who passed the exam" (distributed).

4. No changes needed. Particular Negative (O) proposition; Subject class is "people" (undistributed); Predicate class is "polite individuals who are respected by all" (distributed).

5. Translate to "All political leaders in the United States are persons who interact regularly with the media." Universal Affirmative (A) proposition; Subject class is "political leaders in the United States" (distributed); Predicate class is "persons who interact regularly with the media" (undistributed).

6. Translate to "Some early hard drives for PC computers are things that had only a 10 megabyte capacity." Particular Affirmative (I) proposition; Subject class is "early hard drives for PC computers" (undistributed); Predicate class is "things that had only a 10 megabyte capacity" (undistributed).

7. No changes needed. Universal Negative (E) proposition; Subject class is "pit bulls" (distributed); Predicate class is "animals which can be allowed to run freely in the neighborhood" (distributed).

8. Translate to "Some basketball fans are not people who want a shot clock." Particular negative (O) proposition; Subject class is "basketball fans" (undistributed); Predicate class is "people who want a shot clock" (distributed). NOTE: It is also possible to translate this statement to "Some basketball fans are people who do not want a shot clock." In this case the statement is Particular Affirmative (I); Subject class is "basketball fans" (undistributed); Predicate class is "people who do not want a shot clock" (undistributed).

9. No changes needed. Particular affirmative (I) proposition. Subject class is "influential political supporters of the president" (undistributed); Predicate class is "business people" (undistributed).

10. Translate to "All severe weather warnings are things that are broadcast on radio and television." Universal affirmative (A) proposition; Subject class is "severe weather warnings" (distributed); Predicate class is "things that are broadcast on radio and television." (undistributed).

p. 51–52:

I.

1a   is False

1b   is Unknown

1c   is True

1d   is Unknown

1e   is False

1f   is True

2a   is False

2b   is Unknown

2c   is False

2d   is True

2e   is True

2f   is Unknown

3a   is Unknown

3b   is False

3c   is False

3d   is True

3e   is Unknown

3f   is True

4a   is False

4b   is True

4c   is Unknown

4d   is False

4e   is Unknown

4f   is True

II.   Since logic deals with form, not content, each of the categorical propositions says the same thing regardless of what the S and P stand for. While the content determines whether a given categorical proposition is true or false in fact, the **logical** relationships between and among the propositions are always the same. The contradictories, for example, will always have opposite truth values, so that for **any** A proposition that is true, the **O** will be false, etc.

p. 58:

_____

1. SP = 0 says that the class consisting of what is **both** S and P has no members or is empty: there are no SP's. The diagram shows this by shading the area in the middle which is common to both S and P. In a Venn diagram, shading indicates that there is nothing in that area.

2. The diagrams of the pairs of contradictories say opposite things. Consider the diagrams of the A and the O: the A diagram shades the part of the S circle on the left outside of P, while the O diagram puts an X in this same area. Shading means **nothing** is there, while an x means **something** is there. Thus the A and the O diagrams contradict each other. The same is true of the E and I diagrams: the E diagram shades the middle area which is common to both S and P, while the I diagram puts an X in this same area.

3. Here are the diagrams for the examples suggested in the exercise:

   "No dogs are cats." DC = 0

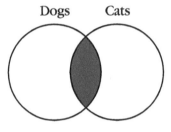

Figure 1

   "Some birds are runners." BR ≠ 0

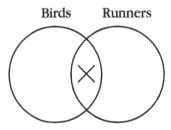

Figure 2

"All logic students study syllogisms."

Translate to: "All logic students are people who study syllogisms." LP = 0

Logic Students   People who study syllogisms

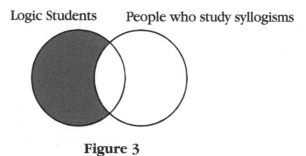

Figure 3

"Some collies do not bark."

Translate to "Some collies are not animals who bark." CA ≠ 0

Collies   Animals who bark

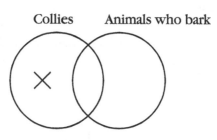

Figure 4

OR, Translate to "Some collies are animals who do not bark." CA ≠ 0

Collies   Animals who do not bark

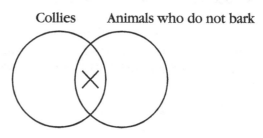

Figure 5

p. 64:

I.   The combination of mood and figure enables us to identify each unique categorical syllogism, e.g. AAA-1 refers to this specific syllogism:

> All M are P
> All S are M
> ∴ All S are P

In the next section, 3.7, we will learn how to test the validity of AAA-1 and all the other categorical syllogisms. AAA-1 is valid, as we will see, and this means that it is always and forever valid. AAA-2, on the other hand, is and always will be invalid. The mood-figure combination, then, gives us each syllogism so that we can then test its validity.

II.

1.   "Some students learn logic easily" is the conclusion, since the word "because" follows it and introduces the premises which give evidence (reasons) for it. Translating this to "Some students are people who learn logic easily," we see that "students" is the minor term and "people who learn logic easily" is the major term." This makes "All people capable of hard work are people who learn logic easily" (appropriately translated) the major premiss, and "Some students are people capable of hard work" (appropriately translated) the minor premiss. The syllogism in standard form, then, is:

> All people capable of hard work are people who learn logic easily.
> Some students are people capable of hard work.
> ∴ Some students are people who learn logic easily.

The mood and figure are AII-1.

2.   The conclusion is "Some logic students are mathematicians." We know this since "and because" occurs after the first statement, telling us that it *and* the statement to follow are both premises. "Logic students" is thus the minor term and "mathematicians" is the major term. This makes "Some people who reason analytically are mathematicians" the major premiss and "All logic students are people who reason analytically" (appropriately translated) the minor premiss. The syllogism in standard form, then, is:

> Some people who reason analytically are mathematicians.
> All logic students are people who reason analytically.
> ∴ Some logic students are mathematicians.

The mood and figure are IAI-1.

3. The conclusion is "Some animals are collies," as shown by the conclusion-indicator "so." "Animals" is thus the minor term and "collies" is the major term. This makes "All collies are dogs" the major premiss and "All dogs are animals" the minor premiss. The syllogism in standard form, then, is:

> All collies are dogs.
> All dogs are animals.
> ∴ Some animals are collies.

The mood and figure are AAI-4.

4. "No computers have minds" is the conclusion, since the word "for" follows it and introduces the premisses which give evidence (reasons) for it. Translating this to "No computers are things that have minds," we see that "computers" is the minor term and "things that have minds" is the major term. This makes "All people are things that have minds" (appropriately translated) the major premiss, and "No computers are people" the minor premiss. The syllogism in standard form, then, is:

> All people are things that have minds.
> No computers are people.
> ∴ No computers are things that have minds.

The mood and figure are AEE-1.

5. "Some children do not make mistakes" is the conclusion, indicated by "so." (Note, however, that inserted between the conclusion-indicator "so" and the conclusion is a comma and then another premiss, indicated by "because.") Translating this to "Some children are not people who make mistakes," we see that "children" is the minor term and "people who make mistakes" is the major term. This makes "All stupid people are people who make mistakes" (appropriately translated) the major premiss, and "Some children are not stupid people" (appropriately translated) the minor premiss. The syllogism in standard form, then, is:

> All stupid people are people who make mistakes.
> Some children are not stupid people.
> ∴ Some children are not people who make mistakes.

The mood and figure are AOO-1.

6. "Some 'just plain folks' are virtuous people" is the conclusion, as shown by the conclusion-indicator "so." "Just plain folks" is thus the minor term and "virtuous people" is the major term. This makes "Some tv stars are virtuous people" the major premiss and "No tv stars are 'just plain folks'" the minor premiss. The syllogism in standard form, then, is:

Some tv stars are virtuous people.
No tv stars are "just plain folks."
∴ Some "just plain folks" are virtuous people.

The mood and figure are IEI-3.

7. "Some dogs are not cats" is the conclusion, since the word "since" follows it and introduces the premisses which give evidence (reasons) for it. "Dogs" is thus the minor term and "cats" is the major term. This makes "No cats are intelligent animals" (appropriately translated) the major premiss and "Some dogs are intelligent animals" (appropriately translated) the minor premiss. The syllogism in standard form, then, is:

No cats are intelligent animals.
Some dogs are intelligent animals.
∴ Some dogs are not cats.

The mood and figure are EIO-2.

pp. 83–84:

I. Following are the seven categorical syllogisms in standard form, with moods, figures, Venn Diagrams, and determination of validity or invalidity.

1. AII-1

All M are P
Some S are M
∴ Some S are P

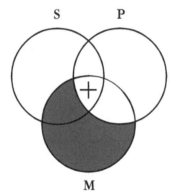

Valid

2. IAI-1

   Some M are P
   All S are M
   ∴ Some S are P

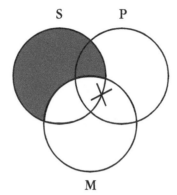

Invalid: Breaks Rule 2

3. AAI-4

   All P are M
   All M are S
   ∴ Some S are P

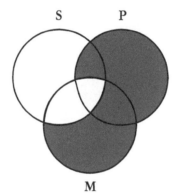

Invalid: Breaks Rule 6

4. AEE-1

   All M are P
   No S are M
   ∴ No S are P

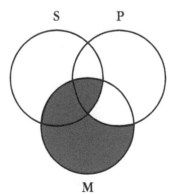

Invalid: Breaks Rule 3

5. AOO-1

All M are P
Some S are not M
∴ Some S are not P

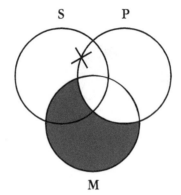

Invalid: Breaks Rule 3

6. IEI-3

Some M are P
No M are S
∴ Some S are P

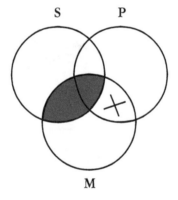

Invalid: Breaks Rule 5

7. EIO-2

No P are M
Some S are M
∴ Some S are not P

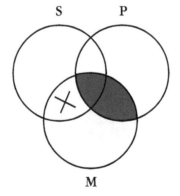

Valid

II:

1. Since the first two letters of OEI-4 are O and E, and since these are both negative propositions, we know from this alone that Rule 4 is broken. Since the third letter is I, we know that OEI has an affirmative conclusion with a negative premiss, breaking Rule 5. Note that we can tell both of these things from the mood alone; the same would be true of OEI in the other three figures.

2. Both premisses of AAI-2 are universal propositions (both A's) and the conclusion is a particular proposition (I), violating Rule 6. This is true for all for figures of AAI.

3. The I proposition does not distribute either of its terms. Since Rule 3 deals only with terms distributed in the conclusion (saying that such terms must also be distributed in the premisses where they appear), any syllogism with an I conclusion can never break Rule 3.

4. The E proposition distributes both terms, so any syllogism with a mood beginning EE will distribute **all** of the terms in its premisses. The middle term, then, will be distributed twice, whereas Rule 2 requires only that it be distributed once. Rule 2, then, will never be broken. However, since E is a negative proposition, a syllogism beginning EE will have two negative premisses, breaking Rule 4.

5. As explained on p. 82 of the text, EEI breaks Rule 4 because its premisses are both negative. It breaks Rule 5 because it has an affirmative conclusion with a negative premiss. It breaks Rule 6 because both of its premisses (EE) are universal and its conclusion (I) is particular.

III. Any of the 256 syllogisms can be chosen. Here are all 15 of the valid syllogisms with their Venn Diagrams; none of these break any Rules. All 241 of the other syllogisms are invalid and will break one or more Rules.

1. AAA-1

   All M are P
   All S are M
   ∴ All S are P

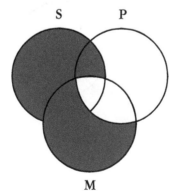

2. AEE-2

All P are M
No S are M
∴ No S are P

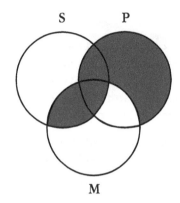

3. AEE-4

All P are M
No M are S
∴ No S are P

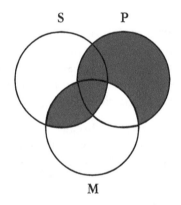

4. AII-1

All M are P
Some S are M
∴ Some S are P

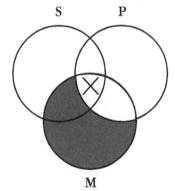

5. AII-3

   All M are P
   Some M are S
   ∴ Some S are P

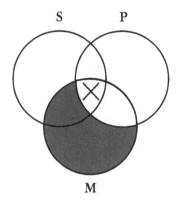

6. AOO-2

   All P are M
   Some S are not M
   ∴ Some S are not P

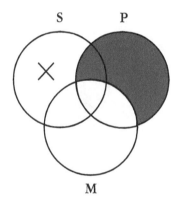

7. EAE-1

   No M are P
   All S are M
   ∴ No S are P

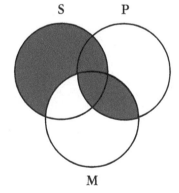

174

8. EAE-2

No P are M
All S are M
∴ No S are P

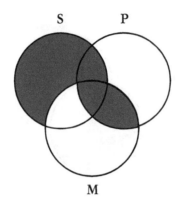

9. EIO-1

No M are P
Some S are M
∴ Some S are not P

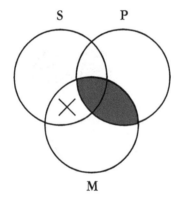

10. EIO-2

No P are M
Some S are M
∴ Some S are not P

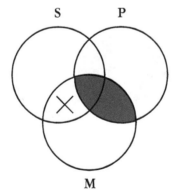

11. EIO-3

No M are P
Some M are S
∴ Some S are not P

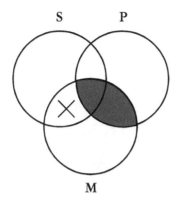

12. EIO-4

No P are M
Some M are S
∴ Some S are not P

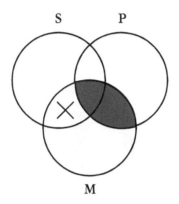

13. IAI-3

Some M are P
All M are S
∴ Some S are P

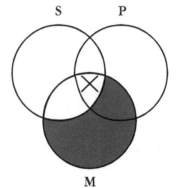

14. IAI-4

Some P are M
All M are S
∴ Some S are P

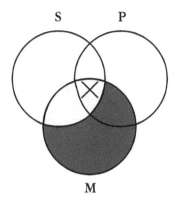

15. OAO-3

Some M are not P
All M are S
∴ Some S are not P

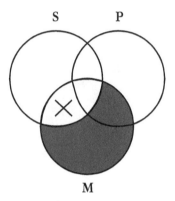

pp. 102–103:

I.

a. Since the only way a conjunction can be true is if both of its conjuncts are true, we know that a conjunction with one false conjunct must be false.

b. Since the only way a disjunction can be false is if both of its disjuncts are false, we know that a disjunction with one true disjunct is true.

c. The negation of any statement has the opposite truth value of that statement. Thus the conjunction of any statement with its own negation will always have one true and one false conjunct. Since a conjunction can only be true if both of its conjuncts are true, a conjunction of any statement with its own negation must be false.

d. The negation of any statement has the opposite truth value of that statement. Thus the disjunction of any statement with its own negation will always have one true and one false disjunct. Since a disjunction can only be false if both of its disjuncts are false, a disjunction of any statement with its own negation must be true.

II. **Note that in these exercises, it is assumed that "U" is the same statement each time it appears.**

1. T

2. F

3. U

4. U

5. T

6. F

7. U

8. T

9. F

10. T

III.

1. ~B v (J · Z)

2. ~(J v D) **or** ~J · ~D

3. J · (B v D)

4. ~J · (B v D)

5. [D · (J v B)] · ~Z

pp. 107–108:

I. "Implies" in the context of symbolic logic refers to material implication and not to other senses of the term in ordinary language. Material implication is a truth function, and by definition any statement of the form p⊃ q (which can be read "p implies q") is true in every case except where **p** (the antecedent) is true and **q** (the consequent) is false. This means that where **p** (the antecedent) is false, the conditional statement

p⊃ q will always be true regardless of the truth value of **q.** This sounds odd only when we read other senses of "implies" into "A false statement implies any statement at all."

II.   **Note that in these exercises, it is assumed that "U" is the same statement each time it appears.**

1. T

2. T

3. T

4. F

5. U

6. T (Note: This is because both antecedent and consequent are the same statement and thus have the same truth value. The same can be said for 3 above.)

7. U

8. T

9. T

10. F

III.

1. P v (R⊃ T)

2. R⊃ (C v G)

3. G⊃ (W v L)

4. (P·W)⊃ T

5. P⊃ (L⊃ ~T)

pp. 117–119, II:

1.

Conclusion		Premiss
p	**q**	**p⊃ q**
T	T	T
T	F	F
F	T	T
F	F	T

The argument form is invalid, since in both the third and fourth line the premiss is true and the conclusion false.

2.

Premiss 2			Premiss 1	Conclusion
p	**q**	**r**	**p⊃ q**	**q v r**
T	T	T	T	T
T	T	F	T	T
T	F	T	F	T
T	F	F	F	F
F	T	T	T	T
F	T	F	T	T
F	F	T	T	T
F	F	F	T	F

The argument form is valid, since there is no line in which both premisses are true and the conclusion false.

3.

p	q	r	Premiss 1 p ⊃ q	Premiss 2 q ⊃ r	Conclusion p ⊃ r
T	T	T	T	T	T
T	T	F	T	F	F
T	F	T	F	T	T
T	F	F	F	T	F
F	T	T	T	T	T
F	T	F	T	F	T
F	F	T	T	T	T
F	F	F	T	T	T

The argument form is valid, since there is no line in which both premisses are true and the conclusion false.

4.

p	Conclusion q	Premiss p ⊃ q
T	T	T
T	F	F
F	T	T
F	F	T

The argument form is invalid, since in the fourth line the premiss is true and the conclusion false.

5.

			Premiss 1	Premiss 2	Conclusion
p	**q**	**p⊃ q**	**~p**	**~q**
T	T	T	F	F
T	F	F	F	T
F	T	T	T	F
F	F	T	T	T

The argument form is invalid, since in the third line both premisses are true and the conclusion false.

6.

Conclusion		Premiss 1	Premiss 2
p	**q**	**p⊃ q**	**~q**
T	T	T	F
T	F	F	T
F	T	T	F
F	F	T	T

The argument form is invalid, because in the fourth line both premisses are true and the conclusion false.

182

7.

p	q	r	Premiss 1 p⊃ q	Premiss 2 q⊃ r	Conclusion r⊃ p
T	T	T	T	T	T
T	T	F	T	F	T
T	F	T	F	T	T
T	F	F	F	T	T
F	T	T	T	T	F
F	T	F	T	F	T
F	F	T	T	T	F
F	F	F	T	T	T

The argument form is invalid, since in both the fifth and seventh lines both premisses are true and the conclusion false.

8.

p	q	r	Conclusion q v r	Premiss 1 p⊃ (q v r)	Premiss 2 ~p
T	T	T	T	T	F
T	T	F	T	T	F
T	F	T	T	T	F
T	F	F	F	F	F
F	T	T	T	T	T
F	T	F	T	T	T
F	F	T	T	T	T
F	F	F	F	T	T

The argument form is invalid, since in the eighth line both premisses are true and the conclusion false.

9.

					Premiss	Conclusion
p	**q**	**r**	**p⊃q**	**q⊃r**	**(p⊃q) v (q⊃r)**	**(p⊃q) · (q⊃r)**
T	T	T	T	T	T	T
T	T	F	T	F	T	F
T	F	T	F	T	T	F
T	F	F	F	T	T	F
F	T	T	T	T	T	T
F	T	F	T	F	T	F
F	F	T	T	T	T	T
F	F	F	T	T	T	T

The argument form is invalid, since in the second, third, fourth, and sixth lines the premiss is true and the conclusion false.

10.

				Premiss 1	Premiss 2	Conclusion
p	**q**	**r**	**p⊃q**	**(p⊃q) · r**	**q⊃r**	**p⊃r**
T	T	T	T	T	T	T
T	T	F	T	F	F	F
T	F	T	F	F	T	T
T	F	F	F	F	T	F
F	T	T	T	T	T	T
F	T	F	T	F	F	T
F	F	T	T	T	T	T
F	F	F	T	F	T	T

The argument form is valid, since there is no line in which both premisses are true and the conclusion false.

III.

> C ⊃ J
> C
> ∴ J v M

This argument is a substitution instance of argument form 2 in Exercises II above (p. 115). Since that argument form is valid, all substitution instances of it are valid. This includes the argument we are presently considering.

IV.   Each of the following arguments is a substitution instance of the argument form with the same number in Exercises II above. Each of those argument forms is the specific form of the argument below with the same number. Those arguments with valid specific forms are themselves valid, and those arguments with invalid specific forms are themselves invalid; thus no new truth tables are needed.

1.   If today is Saturday, then I am happy. Therefore, today is Saturday.

> S ⊃ H
> ∴ S   Invalid

2.   See III above for a substitution instance of this one.

3.   If Fido is a collie, then Fido is a dog. If Fido is a dog, then Fido is an animal. Therefore, if Fido is a collie, then Fido is an animal.

> C ⊃ D
> D ⊃ A
> ∴ C ⊃ A   Valid

4.   If I am a dog, then I am happy. Therefore, I am happy.

> D ⊃ H
> ∴ H   Invalid

5.   If that man is Socrates, then he is a good person. That man is not Socrates. Therefore, he is not a good person.

> S ⊃ G
> ~S
> ∴ ~G   Invalid

6.   If that man is Socrates, then he is a good person. He is not a good person. Therefore, that man is Socrates.

> S ⊃ G
> ~G
> ∴ S   Invalid

7. If that man is Socrates, then he is a good person. If he is a good person, then I respect him. Therefore, if I respect him, then that man is Socrates.

> S⊃ G
> G⊃ R
> ∴ R⊃ S   Invalid

8. If today is Saturday, then I will either sleep late or mow the lawn. Today is not Saturday. Therefore, I will either sleep late or mow the lawn.

> S ⊃ (L v M)
> ~S
> ∴ L v M   Invalid

9. Either my pursuit of pleasure implies that I will have fun, or my having fun implies that I will be happy. Therefore, my pursuit of pleasure implies that I will have fun, and my having fun implies that I will be happy.

> (P⊃ F) v (F ⊃ H)
> ∴ (P⊃ F) · (F ⊃ H)   Invalid

10. If Lassie is a collie, then Lassie is a dog; and Lassie is an animal. If Lassie is a dog, then Lassie is an animal. Therefore, if Lassie is a collie, then Lassie is an animal. *Note: The semicolon and the word "and" both indicate that "Lassie is an animal" is the second conjunct of a conjunction in the first premiss.*

> (C⊃ D) · A
> D⊃ A
> ∴ C⊃ A   Valid

pp. 125–126:

I.   Since the biconditional symbol (≡) always says that the truth value of the statements on both sides of the symbol is the same, all biconditionals claim to be tautologies—that is, they claim to always be true. This is similar to saying that all arithmetic equations using the equal sign (=) claim that the numerical value on both sides of the equal sign is the same. Just as some arithmetic statements using the equal sign are incorrect, however (e.g. 2+3=6), so some biconditionals are not always true. If they are not always true (tautologies) then they must either be never true (self-contradictions) or sometimes true (contingent statements).

II.

1.

		Left conjunct	Right conjunct	
p	**q**	**p⊃ q**	**~(p⊃ q)**	**(p⊃ q) ·~(p⊃ q)**
T	T	T	F	F
T	F	F	T	F
F	T	T	F	F
F	F	T	F	F

Self-contradiction

2.

		Right conjunct	Left conjunct	
p	**q**	**r**	**p⊃ q**	**(p⊃ q) · r**
T	T	T	T	T
T	T	F	T	F
T	F	T	F	F
T	F	F	F	F
F	T	T	T	T
F	T	F	T	F
F	F	T	T	T
F	F	F	T	F

Contingent

3.

		Left side			Right side	
p	**q**	**p⊃ q**	**~q**	**~p**	**~q ⊃ ~p**	**(p⊃ q) ≡ (~q ⊃ ~p)**
T	T	T	F	F	T	T
T	F	F	T	F	F	T
F	T	T	F	T	T	T
F	F	T	T	T	T	T

Tautology

4.

		Antecedent **and** Consequent	
p	**q**	**p⊃ q**	**(p⊃ q) ⊃ (p⊃ q)**
T	T	T	T
T	F	F	T
F	T	T	T
F	F	T	T

Tautology

Note: Some might prefer to make two identical columns for the antecedent and consequent. I have made only one column above since they are the same statement.

188

5.

p	q	r	q · r	Left side p v (q · r)	p · q	p · r	Right side (p · q) v (p · r)	[p v (q·r)] ≡ [(p·q) v (p·r)]
T	T	T	T	T	T	T	T	T
T	T	F	F	T	T	F	T	T
T	F	T	F	T	F	T	T	T
T	F	F	F	T	F	F	F	F
F	T	T	T	T	F	F	F	F
F	T	F	F	F	F	F	F	T
F	F	T	F	F	F	F	F	T
F	F	F	F	F	F	F	F	T

Contingent

6.

p	q	r	q · r	Left side p v (q · r)	p v q	p v r	Right side (p v q) · (p v r)	[p v (q·r)] ≡ [(p v q) ·(p vr)]
T	T	T	T	T	T	T	T	T
T	T	F	F	T	T	T	T	T
T	F	T	F	T	T	T	T	T
T	F	F	F	T	T	T	T	T
F	T	T	T	T	T	T	T	T
F	T	F	F	F	T	F	F	T
F	F	T	F	F	F	T	F	T
F	F	F	F	F	F	F	F	T

Tautology

7.

p	q	Left disjunct	Right disjunct	
		p⊃ q	~(p⊃ q)	(p⊃ q) v~(p⊃ q)
T	T	T	F	T
T	F	F	T	T
F	T	T	F	T
F	F	T	F	T

Tautology

8.

p	q	Antecedent		Consequent	
		p v p	q v q	~(q v q)	(p v p) ⊃ ~(q v q)
T	T	T	T	F	F
T	F	T	F	T	T
F	T	F	T	F	T
F	F	F	F	T	T

*Note: To see that **p v p** produces the same column as **p**, it might be useful to construct a second **p** column. The same goes for **q v q** and **q**.*

Contingent

9.

p	q	Left side			Right side	
		p⊃ q	~q	~q v p	(p⊃ q) ≡ (~q v p)	
T	T	T	F	T	T
T	F	F	T	T	F
F	T	T	F	F	F
F	F	T	T	T	T

Contingent

10.

p	q		Left side side			Right side	
		p v q	~(p v q)	~p	~q	~p · ~q	~(p v q) ≡ (~p · ~q)
T	T	T	F	F	F	F	T
T	F	T	F	F	T	F	T
F	T	T	F	T	F	F	T
F	F	F	T	T	T	T	T

Tautology

pp. 132–133:

I.   The method of formal proof provides a demonstration of the validity of an argument. It therefore can only be used with arguments already known to be valid. The truth table method, on the other hand, can be used to test any argument (or argument form) to determine whether it is valid or invalid.

II.

1. Hypothetical Syllogism (H.S.)

2. Disjunctive Syllogism (D.S.)

3. Constructive Dilemma (C.D.)

4. Modus Tollens (M.T.)

5. Absorption (Abs.)

6. Modus Ponens (M.P.)

7. Simplification (Simp.)

8. Addition (Add.)

9. Modus Ponens (M.P.)

10. Conjunction (Conj.)

Each of the arguments is a substitution instance of the argument form named. Since each of these argument forms has been (or can be) proved valid using a truth table, we know that all substitution instances of them will themselves be valid arguments.

pp. 136–137:

I.

1.

1. A v C

2. C ⊃ D

3. ~A /∴ D

4. C 1, 3, D.S.

5. D 2, 4, M.P.

2.

1. J ⊃ K

2. K ⊃ L

3. ~L /∴ ~J

4. J ⊃ L 1, 2, H.S.

5. ~J 4, 3, M.T.

OR:

1. J ⊃ K

2. K ⊃ L

3. ~L /∴ ~J

4. ~K 2, 3, M.T.

5. ~J 1, 4, M.T.

3.

1. D ⊃ (E v F)

2. G

3. D /∴ (E v F) · G

4. E v F 1, 3, M.P.

5. (E v F) · G 4, 2, Conj.

4.

1. J · (H v I) /∴ J v H

2. J 1, Simp.

3. J v H 2, Add.

5.

1. (A ⊃ B) · (C ⊃ D)

2. A /∴ B v D

3. A v C 2, Add.

4. B v D 1, 3, C.D.

6.

1. J · (K v L)

2. J ⊃ (M · N) /∴ M

3.   J 1, Simp.

4.   M · N 2, 3, M.P.

5.   M 4, Simp.

7.

1.   (W v X) ⊃ (Y · Z)

2.   W /∴ Y

3.   W v X 2, Add.

4.   Y · Z 1, 3, M.P.

5.   Y 4, Simp.

8.

1.   M ⊃ N

2.   (M · N) ⊃ O

3.   M /∴ O

4.   N 1, 3, M.P.

5.   M · N 3, 4, Conj.

6.   O 2,5, M.P.

OR:

1.   M ⊃ N

2.   (M · N) ⊃ O

3.   M /∴ O

4.   M ⊃ (M · N) 1, Abs.

5.   M ⊃ O 4, 2, H.S.

6.   O 5, 3, M.P.

9.

1.   D ⊃ (E v F)

2.   ~ (E v F)

3. ~D ⊃ G /∴ G v E

4. ~D 1,2, M.T.

5. G 3, 4, M.P.

6. G v E 5, Add.

10.

1. A ⊃ B

2. C ⊃ D

3. A /∴ (B v D)

4. A v C 3, Add.

5. (A ⊃ B) · (C ⊃ D) 1, 2, Conj.

6. B v D 5, 4, C.D.

OR:

1. A ⊃ B

2. C ⊃ D

3. A /∴ (B v D)

4. B 1, 3, M.P.

5. B v D 4, Add.

II. Note: In the following arguments, capital letters are used to represent the simple statements making up the premisses and conclusions of the arguments in the book. The choice of letters should be obvious, e.g. "L" for "I can learn logic" and "A" for "I can learn anything." One may, of course, choose other letters.

1.

1. L ⊃ A

2. M v L

3. ~M /∴ A

4. L 2, 3, D.S.

5. A 1, 4, M.P.

2.

   1.   B ⊃ (J ⊃ T)

   2.   ~J ⊃ C

   3.   ~T

   4.   B /∴ C

   5.   J ⊃ T 1, 4, M.P.

   6.   ~J 5, 3, M.T.

   7.   C 2, 6, M.P.

3.

   1.   B ⊃ J

   2.   M ⊃ T

   3.   B v M

   4.   ~J /∴ T

   5.   (B ⊃ J) · (M ⊃ T) 1, 2, Conj.

   6.   J v T 5, 3, C.D.

   7.   T 6, 4, D.S.

4.

   1.   (L ⊃ F) · (W ⊃ M)

   2.   F ⊃ E /∴ L ⊃ E

   3.   L ⊃ F 1, Simp.

   4.   L ⊃ E 3, 2, H.S.

5.

   1.   C v (L ⊃ P)

   2.   ~C

   3.   L /∴ P

   4.   L ⊃ P 1,2, D.S.

   5.   P 4, 3, M.P.

pp. 140–141:

I. Any **statement** may be replaced by a logically equivalent **statement** wherever it occurs, whether in a whole line or part of a line. (A⊃ **B,** for example, can be replaced by **~A v B,** since this is a substitution instance of the logical equivalence called Material Implication.) On the other hand, the first nine Rules of Inference are valid **argument forms,** and any substitution instance of one of them is itself a valid **argument.** A **whole line** of a proof follows (as a conclusion) from one or more **whole lines** (as premisses) as a substitution instance of one of these argument forms. If two lines of an argument read **A⊃ B** and **A** respectively, then **B** follows since this is a substitution instance of **modus ponens.**

II. Note: In several of these arguments in the next two sets of exercises, there are other ways to arrive at the conclusion. The steps can often be done in a different order, or different substitutions can be made. All of the proofs below work, but the reader is invited to try other ways.

1.

   1.   A ⊃ (~B v C)

   2.   (B ⊃ C) ⊃ D /∴ A ⊃ D

   3.   A ⊃ (B ⊃ C) 1, Impl.

   4.   A ⊃ D 3, 2, H.S.

2.

   1.   J · (K · L) /∴ K

   2.   (K · L) · J 1, Com.

   3.   K · L 2, Simp.

   4.   K 3, Simp.

3.

   1.   C v ~~D

   2.   ~C /∴ D

   3.   ~~D 1,2, D.S.

   4.   D 3, D.N.

4.

    1. $(\sim K \supset \sim L) \supset (M \vee M)$

    2. $L \supset K$ /∴ M

    3. $(L \supset K) \supset (M \vee M)$ 1, Trans.

    4. $M \vee M$ 3,2, M.P.

    5.   M 4, Taut.

5.

    1. $(W \vee V) \supset \sim (X \vee Y)$

    2.   W /∴ $\sim X$

    3. $W \vee V$ 2, Add.

    4. $\sim (X \vee Y)$ 1, 3, M.P.

    5. $\sim X \cdot \sim Y$ 4, De M.

    6. $\sim X$ 5, Simp.

6.

    1. $X \vee (Y \cdot Z)$

    2. $\sim X$ /∴ Z

    3. $Y \cdot Z$ 1, 2, D.S.

    4. $Z \cdot Y$ 3, Com.

    5.   Z 4, Simp.

7.

    1. $C \supset D$

    2. $D \supset C$ /∴ $C \equiv D$

    3. $(C \supset D) \cdot (D \supset C)$ 1, 2, Conj.

    4. $C \equiv D$ 3, Equiv.

8.

   1.   A ⊃ ~ (B v C)

   2.   A /∴ ~B

   3.   ~ (B v C) 1,2, M.P.

   4.   ~B · ~C 3, De M.

   5.   ~B 4, Simp.

9.

   1.   (J · K) ⊃ (L v M) /∴ J ⊃ [K ⊃ (L v M)]

   2.   J ⊃ [K ⊃ (L v M)] 1, Exp.

10.

   1.   (A · B) v (A · C) /∴ A

   2.   A · (B v C) 1, Dist.

   3.   A 2, Simp.

III. Note: In the following arguments, capital letters are used to represent the simple statements making up the premises and conclusions of the arguments in the book. The choice of letters should be obvious, e.g., "A" for "John attends class," "P" for "He will pass the course," and "G" for "He will graduate."

1.

   1.   ~ A ⊃ ~P

   2.   A ⊃ G

   3.   P /∴ G

   4.   P ⊃ A 1, Trans.

   5.   P ⊃ G 4, 2, H.S.

   6.   G 5, 3, M.P.

2.

   1.   (B v F) ⊃ L

   2.   F

3.   L ⊃ C /∴ C

4.   F v B 2, Add.

5.   B v F 4, Com.

6.   L 1, 5, M.P.

7.   C 3, 6, M.P.

3.

1.   (M v B) ⊃ ~(J v T)

2.   M /∴ ~J

3.   M v B 2, Add.

4.   ~(J v T) 1, 3, M.P.

5.   ~J · ~T 4, De M.

6.   ~J 5, Simp.

4.

1.   ~L v V

2.   L /∴ V v M

3.   ~~L 2, D.N.

4.   V 1,3, D.S.

5.   V v M 4, Add.

5.

1.   (Y v I) ⊃ C

2.   ~C /∴ ~Y

3.   ~(Y v I) 1,2, M.T.

4.   ~Y·~I 3, De M.

5.   ~Y 4, Simp.

200

p. 143:

---

1. C = F, D= T or F, E = T
2. J = T, K = T
3. X = F, Y = F, Z = F
4. P = T, Q = T, R = F
5. J and K= either or both false, L = T

p. 147:

I.   Quantification theory enables us to combine the strengths of both categorical and symbolic logic. Like categorical logic, we can deal with the internal logical structure of statements using quantification theory. But like symbolic logic, we can state and prove the validity of arguments made up of several whole statements.

II.

1. Bs
2. (x)(Cx⊃Fx)
3. (∃x)(Dx · Bx)
4. Cf
5. (x)(Lx⊃ ~Nx)
6. (∃x)(Cx · ~Lx)
7. (∃x)(Cx · Lx)
8. Og
9. (x) (Gx ⊃ Ox)
10. Lj

More Exercises for Practice

In this section, we present several more exercises and hints for most of the sections of exercises found in the book. Unless otherwise indicated, the instructions for each set of exercises are the same as for the corresponding ones in the book.

Chapter One

p. 11, II:

1. The meeting will come to order. (Said by the person chairing the meeting.)

2. Did the meeting come to order?

3. I will soon call the meeting to order.

4. (Secretary to Chairperson): Please call the meeting to order.

p. 22, II:

1. True or False: "The present governor of our state is a former state senator," is a sentence which expresses a *different* statement every time a different person becomes governor of our state.

2. True or False: A deductive argument can have all true premises and a false conclusion and still be valid.

3. If a *valid* deductive argument has all true premises, then: (a) it has a true conclusion but is not necessarily sound; (b) it may or may not have a true conclusion and may or may not be sound; (c) it has a true conclusion and is sound.

4. True or False: A deductive argument can have all true premisses and a true conclusion and yet be *invalid.*

5. True or False: Inductive arguments only claim that their conclusions probably follow from their premisses.

---------------------------------- ----------------------------------

Chapter Two

pp. 36–37, I:

1. (Teenager before prom): "I'm so nervous—I'm either gonna have a great time or I'm gonna die!"

2. Mother said Billy you surprise me.

3. (Line from old toothpaste commercial): "Ultra-Brite gives your mouth sex appeal!"

4. Why is everyone always trying to trick me?

5. (Letter from bill collector): We hope that you will pay your bill immediately. We would like to avoid having to take any further action.

6. I'm really anxious to hear the speaker from the White House who's coming to our school today. He must be really important to work there!

7. (Children's rhyme while walking on a sidewalk): If you step on a crack, you'll break your Mother's back!

8. I'm really glad they raised the speed limit to 65 mph on this road, but that stretch of highway up ahead is a little narrow. I'll be very careful as I drive through that stretch at 65!

9. The mechanic said he needs to "true" the brakes on my car. I guess I'd better let him do it—I sure wouldn't want false brakes!

10. I told you that these are the rules of this game. Why are these the rules? Because I told you.

---------------------------------- ----------------------------------

Chapter Three

p. 44, II:

1. All dogs wag their tails.

2. Some people have too much time on their hands.

3. No detail-oriented people are big-picture people.

4. Some highly intelligent computer designers lack common sense.
   (Hint: Depending on how the predicate class is designated, this one can be translated as either an I or an O proposition; it is similar to #8 on p. 44.)

pp. 51–52:

These exercises cover all of the relationships on the traditional square of opposition. For further practice, try mixing them up a bit: pick a random proposition and designate it either "true" or "false." Then determine the truth value of the other three propositions. For further practice, take a proposition, give it a truth value, and ask about its converse, obverse, or contrapositive. The answer always will be "true," "false," or "undetermined."

p. 64:

It is easy to come up with more syllogisms. Make up an argument which is a categorical syllogism, being sure to put it in standard form, e.g.:

> All virtuous people are good citizens.
> Some rock stars are virtuous people.
> Therefore, some rock stars are good citizens.

It is easy to name the mood and figure of this argument (AII-1) when it is stated this way. Now try stating it in different orders, using premiss-indicators or conclusion-indicators, e.g.:

Some rock stars are good citizens, **because (or since, or for)** all virtuous people are good citizens and some rock stars are virtuous people. (Similar to 1, 4, and 7 on p. 64)

All virtuous people are good citizens, **so (or therefore, or hence)** some rock stars are good citizens, **since (or because, or for)** some rock stars are virtuous people. (Similar to 3 and 6 on p. 64)

All virtuous people are good citizens, **and since (or because)** some rock stars are virtuous people, some rock stars are good citizens. (Similar to 2 on p. 64)

Some rock stars are virtuous people, **so (or therefore, or hence), since (or because)** all virtuous people are good citizens, some rock stars are good citizens. (Similar to 5 on p. 64)

p. 83–84:

Any categorical syllogism can be tested by the two methods described in the book (Venn Diagrams and Rules). Of the 256 categorical syllogisms, only 15 of them are valid. Of these 15, several share the same Venn Diagram. The 15 valid categorical syllogisms, with their diagrams, appear on pp. 13-18. None of these, of course, break any rules. **All** 241 of the others break at least one rule.

Chapter Four

pp. 102–103, II:

---

*Note: All the exercises for this section in the book presuppose that the unknown statement U is the **same** statement each time it occurs. For additional practice, consider the following exercises in which there are **two different** unknown statements, U and N. This means, of course, that the truth values of U and N are completely independent of each other. Statements T and F, of course, are still true and false respectively. What, then, would be the truth value of the following statements—true, false, or unknown?*

1. N v U

2. N ·~N

3. N ·~U

4. T v (U ·N)

5. F · (U v N)

6. N v ~U

7. ~N · U

8. N v T

9. (U v F) · (F · N)

10. (U v T) v (F v N)

pp. 107–108, II:

*Note: All the exercises for this section in the book presuppose that the unknown statement **U** is the **same** statement each time it occurs. For additional practice, consider the following exercises in which there are **two different** unknown statements, **U** and **N**. This means, of course, that the truth values of **U** and **N** are completely independent of each other. Statements **T** and **F**, of course, are still true and false respectively. What, then, would be the truth value of the following statements—true, false, or unknown?*

1. F ⊃ (U v N)

2. (U · N) ⊃ T

3. (U · N) ⊃ (T v N)

4. (U v N) ⊃ (U v N)

5. (U v N) · (U v N)

6. (U v N) ·~ (U v N)

7. (F v U) ⊃ (T v N)

8. (F · U) ⊃ (T · N)

9. [(U v N) · T] ⊃ T

10. [(U v N) · T] ⊃ F

pp. 117–118, II:

*Note: It is easy to make up more of these argument forms on your own and test them for validity using truth tables. All the exercises in the book are argument forms with either one or two premisses and with either two or three statement variables. For extra practice, make up a few with three or more premisses. The technique is the same. The argument form will be valid **unless** there is one or more row(s) in which **all** the premisses are true and the conclusion false. For further practice, make up some argument forms with four statement variables instead of three (i.e. **p, q, r, and s**). The table for the four statement variables will look like this:*

p	q	r	s
T	T	T	T
T	T	T	F
T	T	F	T
T	T	F	F
T	F	T	T
T	F	T	F
T	F	F	T
T	F	F	F
F	T	T	T
F	T	T	F
F	T	F	T
F	T	F	F
F	F	T	T
F	F	T	F
F	F	F	T
F	F	F	F

Here is a sample argument form with three premisses:

p ∨ q
q ⊃ r
p
∴ r

And here is a sample argument form with four statement variables:

(p ⊃ q) · (r ⊃ s)
p ∨ r
∴ q ∨ s

pp. 125–126, II:

---

*Note: As with argument forms above, it is easy to make up a statement form and use a truth table to discover whether it is a tautology, a self-contradiction, or contingent. For further practice, try some statement forms with four variables (**p, q, r, and s**). The table for four statement variables would be as above. A few sample statement forms with four variables would be as follows:*

1. (p v q) ⊃ (r ·s)

2. [(p v q) v (r · s)] ≡ [(s · r) v (q v p)]

3. [(p ·q) ⊃ (r v s)] ·~[(p ·q) ⊃ (r v s)]

Chapter Five

p. 133, II:

Note: Here are nine more arguments—each is a substitution instance of one of the nine basic argument forms which appear on p. 132. Identify.

1.

> J v K
> K ⊃ M
> ∴ (J v K) ·(K⊃ M)

2.

> [A · (B⊃ C)] v (D ·E)
> ~[A · (B⊃ C)]
> ∴ D ·E

3.

> (P · Q) ⊃ R
> ∴ (P · Q) ⊃ [(P · Q) · R]

4.

    D ⊃ (E v F)
    (E v F) ⊃ G
    ∴ D⊃ G

5.

    [(J ⊃ K) v L] ·(M v N)
    ∴ (J ⊃ K) v L

6.

    ~C ⊃ (D v E)
    ~C
    ∴ D v E

7.

    (A v B) ⊃ (D ·E)
    ~(D ·E)
    ∴ ~(A v B)

8.

    [A ⊃ (B ·C)] ·[D ⊃ (E · F)]
    A v D
    ∴ (B ·C) v (E ·F)

9.

    (X · Y) ⊃ Z
    ∴ [(X · Y) ⊃ Z] v (A · B)

pp. 135–136, I:

Note: The following arguments, like the ones in the book, are valid. They can be proved valid using the nine Rules of Inference (p. 132). No more than three steps beyond the premisses is required in any of the proofs.

1.

    ~(C ·D)
    A ⊃ (C ·D)
    ~A⊃ E /∴ E

2.

> D v (E ⊃ F)
> ~D
> E /∴ F v G

3.

> X ⊃ Y
> (X · Y) ⊃ Z /∴ X ⊃ Z

4.

> A ⊃ B
> C ⊃ D
> A v C /∴ B v D

5.

> F · (G v ~H)
> F ⊃ G /∴ G v ~H

p. 140, II:

Note: The following arguments, like the ones in the book, are valid. They can be proved valid using the nine Rules of Inference (p. 132) along with the logical equivalencies listed with the Rule of Replacement (p. 138). No more than three steps beyond the premisses is required in any of the proofs.

1.

> (A · B) ⊃ C
> B · A /∴ C

2.

> D ⊃ ~ (E v F)
> (~E · ~F) ⊃ G /∴ D ⊃ G

3.

    A ⊃ B
    ~~A /∴ B

4.

    A v (B · C) /∴ A v B

5.

    J v (K ⊃ L)
    ~J /∴ ~K v L

p. 143, II:

Note: A good way to practice this method is to review some of the invalid arguments from pp. 117-118 (1,4,5,6,7,8, and 9 are all invalid). Note the line(s) of the truth tables which made these arguments invalid. This line or lines show the specific truth values which make the premisses all true and the conclusion false. As an example, consider #8 on p. 118:

    p ⊃ (q v r)
    ~p
    ∴ q v r

The truth values which make both premisses true and the conclusion false is:

    p =F
    q=F
    r =F

(This was the eighth line of the truth table for this argument.)

p. 147, II:

---

1. Lassie is intelligent.

2. Some dogs are not intelligent.

3. All dogs are domestic animals.

4. No tigers are domestic animals.

5. Some tigers are zoo animals.